ANCIENT HISTORY

Ancient History

EVIDENCE AND MODELS

M. I. Finley

ELISABETH SIFTON BOOKS
VIKING

ELISABETH SIFTON BOOKS · VIKING
Viking Penguin Inc.
40 West 23rd Street,
New York, New York 10010, U.S.A.

First American Edition
Published in 1986

Library of Congress Cataloging in Publication Data
Finley, M. I. (Moses I.), 1912–
Ancient history.
"Elisabeth Sifton books."
Includes index.
1. Greece—Historiography.   2. Rome—Historiography.
3. History—Research.   I. Title.
DE8.F55   1986   938'.0072   85-40616
ISBN 0-670-80970-5

Printed in Great Britain by
Redwood Burn Ltd, Trowbridge, Wiltshire
Set in Linotron Palatino

To

Peter Garnsey

and

Dick Whittaker

Contents

Preface

This is a book about the study and understanding of the history of the Greeks and Romans; about the evidence that is available to the historians and its severe limitations; about the practices of historians in dealing with the evidence, and about alternative procedures that might be attempted; in sum, about what we can know and what we are unlikely ever to know.

I have been teaching ancient history to university students in the United States and Britain for half a century. Inevitably I have given thought to the nature of this activity, and in recent years I have written a few essays expressing some of those thoughts. This is the first time that I have assembled them in a more systematic way. The occasion was provided by the series of lectures I gave in November 1983 as the J. H. Gray Lectures under the auspices of the Faculty of Classics of the University of Cambridge. With revisions they comprise chapters 2, 4 and 5 of the volume, to which I have added three other chapters originating in different contexts. Chapter 5 was also delivered in German in the universities of Basel and Munich (there together with chapter 4), and in Italian at the Istituto Gramsci in Rome and at the University of Pisa, all in 1984.

I am most grateful to my various hosts, in Cambridge and abroad, for many kindnesses while the lectures were in progress. I must also thank a number of friends who read portions of the manuscript or helped in other ways: in Cambridge Paul Cartledge, John Crook, Peter Garnsey, Garry Runciman and Dick Whittaker; Tony Andrewes in Oxford; Jürgen von Ungern-Sternberg in Basel; Wilfried Nippel and Andreas Wittenburg in Munich; Nino Ampolo and Pino Pucci in Rome; Riccardo Di Donato in Pisa. I am grateful, not for the first time, to Douglas Matthews for the index. And, as with all the books I have produced in these past thirty-odd years, I thank my wife once again for her encouragement and her forbearance.

Darwin College, Cambridge   M.I.F.

[1]

'Progress' in Historiography[1]

In a book on the writing of history, a superlatively clever and
aphoristic work that produced something of an *éclat* when it
appeared in 1971, Paul Veyne wrote that 'Thucydides would
have learned from reading what Burckhardt and Nilsson had
written about his own civilization and his own religion. Had he
himself tried to discuss those topics, his phrases would have been
much poorer than ours.'[2] The curious coupling of Burckhardt and
Nilsson, analogues to coupling Max Weber (or even Arnold
Toynbee) and Langer's *Encyclopedia of World History*, raises
doubts. Nevertheless, beneath the flawed example there lies an
important doctrine, the Crocean view, in Veyne's formulation,
that 'the *intelligence* of history has been enriched from the time of
the Greeks to today, not because we know the principles or the
ends of human events but because we have acquired a much
richer casuistic of these events. That is the only progress of which
historiography is capable' – progress in 'simple description without method'.[3] Elsewhere Veyne speaks of the 'inventory', of the
historian's 'palette', and again of 'conceptualization'. 'Herodotus
and Thucydides had at their disposal all the facts necessary for
founding social history or religious history . . . which they did
not found. It was the "intellectual instruments" that were
lacking.'[4]

In one formulation or another, the Croce-Veyne doctrine
would, I believe, receive widespread assent among historians
today, with no doubt heavier stress on improvements in technique. The implications, however, are not fully drawn out,
perhaps not even recognized. Historians, like members of other
professions (if I may thus class historians), are reluctant to
analyse themselves and their activity: they leave that to the
philosophers, whose efforts they then dismiss as ignorant or

irrelevant or both. In this book, we shall have frequent occasion to look at the implications.[5]

'It is perfectly obvious', it was once said to me, that 'the whole field of social history' – by way of example – 'has been vastly transformed in recent decades.' Is that really the case in the field of ancient history? In several respects, undoubtedly:

1 – The volume of data, the mere numbers of known facts, increase daily with the discovery and publication of hitherto unknown inscriptions, papyri, coins, and occasionally literary texts, and with the still continuing acceleration in archaeological exploration.

2 – Techniques are improving all the time, by the application of modern science in archaeology, by the use of the computer in lexicography, and so on. Today we can date documents and texts with a precision that neither Thucydides nor Burckhardt could have managed, and we can graphically expose Thucydides' choice of words, phrases and syntax as he himself could not have dreamed of.

However, only in the most naive sense could the 'whole field' of social (or political or religious) history be said to have been 'transformed' by either improved techniques or a greater volume of data, or by both together. Thucydides would have learned thousands of facts about his own religion from Martin Nilsson's books, but it is to be doubted that he would have significantly altered his views about the place of religion in history as a result, and it is strenuously to be denied that his 'phrases' would have been 'much poorer' than Nilsson's on the subject. What could be 'poorer' than the following characteristic generalizations by Nilsson: 'the fate of religion is determined by the masses'; 'it was only natural' that women 'should apply to divinities of their own sex'; discussions of religion by the Sophists belong to 'philosophy and must be passed over in an exposition of popular religion'?[6]

3 – Every historian suffers inevitably from ignorance of what will happen after him. Every historian, even the most mediocre, therefore has greater 'historical experience' than his predecessors, however outstanding. That is a truism but it is important. The point is not the banal one that new institutions arise in the

course of 'historical experience'; hence no fifth-century BC Greek could have conceived the Weberian doctrine of bureaucracy. The point is rather that subsequent experience makes possible, and stimulates, a reappraisal of older institutions within their own time and their own context. Had Thucydides known the history of Roman and later religions, he would no doubt have retained his contempt for oracles and their purveyors but he might well have treated the role of religious institutions differently and at greater length (religious institutions, not gods, I hasten to add). Burckhardt, in other words, might have influenced his assessment of his own religion as Nilsson would not. Hindsight is an essential tool of the historian, not a vulgar joke at his expense.

4 – The corollary of accumulating historical experience is a change, or at least a possible change, in stresses and explanatory models. Burckhardt's most brilliant 'discovery' was the central place of the *agon* in Greek life (an untranslatable word, normally rendered by the pale 'athletic competition' or by 'struggle', neither of which captures the overtones as well as its English descendant, 'agony'). I write 'discovery' in inverted commas because all thinking Greeks knew it simply from the absence of the *agon* in other cultures with which they were in direct contact: witness Herodotus on Egypt (2.91) or Lucian's *Anacharsis*. But no Greek gave it the stress, the centrality, it possesses in Burckhardt's *Griechische Kulturgeschichte*.

More than a generation separates Burckhardt from Nilsson, yet, if I am right, the 'transformation' in this instance has been retrogressive. Nor is that all. Hardly any professional ancient historians today read the *Griechische Kulturgeschichte* (or if they do, they fail to acknowledge it), as if Wilamowitz's notorious dismissal of the work – 'for science it doesn't exist'[7] – has become a binding law. Nilsson, on the other hand, is hailed as the greatest twentieth-century authority on ancient Greek religion; the footnotes in most books on the subject abundantly attest his eminence. That there is a positive correlation here between intellectual calibre and professional repute cannot be maintained by even the most severe critic of Burckhardt. Something much more fundamental is involved – about the nature and condition of historiography not merely about two individuals.

A more complex instance is provided by Theodor Mommsen, the *Meister* of Roman history, unrivalled in his own day and today. In 1902 he received the Nobel Prize for Literature, and the main ground for the award was his multi-volume history of Rome, an early work which has met with an equivocal response, or worse, in the profession ever since its publication. The 'strong resonance in the broad reading-public' was accompanied by a 'peevish rejection by many colleagues'.[8] In our own day an eminent ancient historian declared Mommsen's Roman history to be a puzzling work because it introduces the reader 'simultaneously to *two* pasts, to the time of the Romans and to the era of the political struggles of the nineteenth century'. So Hermann Bengtson, in the short introductory chapter to his own *Grundriss der römischen Geschichte* (Sketch of Roman History), published in 1967 in the distinguished series he edited for many years, the *Handbuch der Altertumswissenschaft*, for a century the recognized codification of the state of knowledge in all branches of classical studies (implicit in the word 'Handbook' in the title). Better two pasts than none, it is tempting to retort, but I shall confine myself to the implicit illusion that Bengtson's brand of positivism, his determination to be factual and nothing but factual, is less deeply rooted in his own twentieth century than was Mommsen's 'political pedagogy' in the nineteenth.[9] The mere allocation of space, the ineradicable series of imperial reigns as the containers of post-Republican Roman history, the loud silences on great chunks of human behaviour are proof enough that 'objectivity', freedom from 'subjective values', is pure illusion. The barest bones of any historical narrative, the events selected and arranged in a temporal sequence, imply a value judgment (or judgments).

The study and writing of history, in short, is a form of ideology. That blunt statement will shock, and I must make my meaning explicit. I speak of ideology neither in one of its doctrinal senses (Marx's, for example, or Mannheim's) nor in the familiar sense of the legitimation and support of a system or institution ('the ideology of Augustus') – all to be found in some historical writing

– but in the broadest, 'neutral' sense, roughly as defined in the *Shorter Oxford English Dictionary*: 'a system of ideas concerning phenomena, esp. those of social life; the manner of thinking characteristic of a class or an individual'. Hence I do not equate the ideology of professional historians, at least not of most of them, with the crude, politically motivated distortions, falsifications and suppressions that marked what passed for Italian history throughout the Mussolini era or that converted Trotsky into a non-person in Soviet historiography.

If that is correct, then much of the answer to the question, May we speak of progress in historiography, and, if so, in what sense?, is self-evident. Ideologies change, and so the writing of history undergoes constant 'transformation'. It always has: in antiquity itself one need only remember the sequence Herodotus-Thucydides-Polybius-Livy-Tacitus-Dio Cassius. But progress is a value-judgment, which in this instance rests on one's judgment of the historian's ideology. If, for example, one believes it to be a misjudgment of social behaviour to seek the mainsprings in the personalities and decisions of political and military elites, then the alternative analyses and explanations of some contemporary historians represent progress. Improvements in technique seem to me a minor side-issue in this context. So, to a large extent, is the distinction between narrative history and some other kind, whether the latter is called structural or serial or quantitative or cliometric. It is either another distinction in technique or a concentration on certain phenomena because they lend themselves to new, sophisticated methods.

Professionalism for its own sake, the cult of Research, is an ideological stance, too. If no ingredient, no 'theory', is added, no serious concern with the broad canvas of the past is advanced, nor is fundamental change illuminated. Everything becomes mere contingency. The tone might be called a modified Panglossism: all change is for the worse in the best of all possible worlds, except change in the historian's own technique – progress in 'simple description without method'.

It will be apparent that I retain a rather old-fashioned notion of history as a systematic account over a long enough period of time

5

not only to establish relationships, connections, causes and consequences but also to show how change occurs and to suggest why. Unhappily I cannot agree that the old distinction between antiquarianism and historiography has lost its point, that a 'new notion' of human development has in actual practice 'left little space for mere descriptions of the past'.[10] I cannot agree when, for example, the author of a large-scale 'essay in historical interpretation' of the Roman emperors at work boasts that he has not 'contaminated the presentation of the evidence from the Roman empire with conceptions drawn from wider sociological studies'.[11] That is a recipe for what Momigliano has called 'the antiquarian mentality with its fondness for classification and irrelevant detail'. A historical interpretation is a complex of answers to questions. The evidence propounds no questions. The historian himself does that, and he now possesses an adequate array of concepts for the construction of hypotheses and explanatory models.

[2]

The Ancient Historian
and his Sources[1]

In an account of the evidence for the history of Mesopotamian social organization, Joan Oates introduced her second section, from about 3100 BC, with the simple statement, 'Our knowledge of social structure in Mesopotamia increases exponentially with the invention of writing'.[2] To anyone not involved in the study, it then comes as a shock to discover that this exponential increase in information is not unambiguously welcomed, at least not in the last decade or two, following the emergence of the 'new archaeology'. The happy days are gone when historians of antiquity (whether Near Eastern or Graeco-Roman) could relegate archaeology to a minor ancillary activity that produced picturesque information about private life and art with which to dress up the 'real' history derived from written evidence. The ancient historian today has to accept that his armoury includes qualitatively different kinds of evidence which often appear mutually contradictory or at least unrelated.

What is to be done? I believe that the nature and uses of the evidence about antiquity are being debated more widely and determinedly today than at any time since, say, the days of Boeckh and Niebuhr in the early nineteenth century. Partly this is a consequence of the exponential increase in the quantity of available archaeological information and in the quantity of publication generally in ancient studies, and partly it reflects new approaches to the study of history, new interests and the formulation of new questions. The discussion is wholly to be welcomed in principle, though in practice too much of it reads like a trades union demarcation dispute.

I begin with a point so elementary that it borders on the commonplace. In the words of Momigliano writing about literary, but non-documentary, sources: 'The whole modern method

7

of historical research is founded upon the distinction between original and derivative authorities . . . We praise the original authorities – or sources – for being reliable, but we praise non-contemporary historians – or derivative authorities – for display-ing sound judgment in the interpretation and evaluation of the original sources. This distinction . . . became the common patri-mony of historical research only in the late seventeenth century.'[3]

The last sentence is critical: not only mediaeval historians and pre-eighteenth-century modern historians paid little attention to the distinction between primary and derivative sources; so did the historians in antiquity. A few, notably Herodotus and Thucydides, distinguished between eye-witnesses who could be carefully cross-questioned and all later testimony that was beyond such personal control,[4] but they failed to develop tech-niques of source criticism or ways of dealing satisfactorily with derivative authorities. Of course any idiot could have differen-tiated between a primary and a secondary source, and also between a careful writer and a charlatan; and most historians in antiquity, even the weaker ones, were not idiots. Yet a Livy or a Plutarch cheerfully repeated pages upon pages of earlier accounts over which they neither had nor sought any control. Something other than intelligence was involved, which in the end must come down to a radically different notion from ours of the nature and purpose of the historical exercise. Only Thucydides fully and systematically acknowledged the existence of a dilemma, which he resolved in the unsatisfactory way of refusing to deal with pre-contemporary history at all.[5]

The modern historian of antiquity cannot simply repeat the ancient practice. He cannot write a history of Rome by reworking in a modern language the Latin of Livy as Livy had paraphrased or translated the Greek of Polybius. The 'common patrimony of historical research' that arose at the end of the seventeenth century has made that procedure unacceptable. But that patri-mony, it must be added, seems not to interfere seriously with the practice of 'rescuing' Livy and the rest by rewriting their accounts, rather than just repeating or paraphrasing; a rewriting that ends by tacitly accepting the essential veracity of the original.

Unfortunately, the two longest ancient accounts of Roman Republican history, the area in which the problems are currently the most acute and the most widely discussed, the histories of Livy and of Dionysius of Halicarnassus, were composed about 500 years (in very round numbers) later than the traditional date for the founding of the Republic, 200 years from the defeat of Hannibal. Try as we may, we cannot trace any of their written sources back beyond about 300 B C, and mostly not further than to the age of Marius and Sulla. Yet the early centuries of the Republic and the still earlier centuries that preceded it are narrated in detail in Livy and Dionysius of Halicarnassus. Where did they find their information? No matter how many older statements we can either document or posit – irrespective of possible reliability – we eventually reach a void. But ancient writers, like historians ever since, could not tolerate a void, and they filled it in one way or another, ultimately by pure invention.

The ability of the ancients to invent and their capacity to believe are persistently underestimated.[6] How else could they have filled the blatant gaps in their knowledge once erudite antiquarians had observed that centuries had elapsed between the destruction of Troy and the 'foundation' of Rome, other than by inventing an Alban king-list to bridge the gap? Or how could they contest an existing account other than by offering an alternative, for example, to provide ideological support for, or hostility to, a particular ethnic group, such as Etruscans or Sabines, who played a major role in early Roman history?[7] No wonder that, even in the hopelessly fragmentary state of the surviving material on early Rome, there is a bewildering variety of versions, a variety that continued to increase and multiply as late as the early Principate.[8]

Presumably no one today believes the *Alban* king-list to be anything but a fiction, but any suggestion that there is insufficient ground to give credence to the *Roman* king-list is greeted with outraged cries of 'hyper-criticism' and 'shades of Ettore Pais'. Such epithets do not meet the issues. To begin with, a 250-year period occupied continuously by only seven kings is a demographic improbability, perhaps an impossibility: the first seven emperors under the Principate reigned for a total of one

9

hundred years. Then, to conclude about the second king, Numa Pompilius, that the 'only historical fact' about him is his name and that his biography is 'legendary',[9] is effectively to remove one of the seven from the record. And so on almost *ad infinitum*: it is our incurable weakness that we completely and absolutely lack primary literary sources for Roman history down to about 300 BC and that we have very few available to us for another century. So did Livy and the other later Roman writers (apart from a handful of miscellaneous and often unintelligible documents).

That is unchallengeable as a simple matter of definition. It is then a strange aberration when a reputable Roman historian, writing the volume on the early Romans and Etruscans (down to 390 BC), in a series edited by an equally reputable colleague, prints an appendix headed 'primary sources' which consists of thumbnail sketches in four to ten lines each of a dozen writers, ranging in time from Timaeus, whose long career spanned the end of the fourth century BC and the first half of the third, to Festus, who flourished about AD 150.[10] I cannot imagine that, even as a slip, a Renaissance historian would compile a list of primary sources made up of John Addington Symonds, Burckhardt and Chabod. I suspect that Ogilvie's slip reflects, no doubt unconsciously, the widespread sentiment that anything written in Greek or Latin is somehow privileged, exempt from the normal canons of evaluation.

The insufficiency of primary literary sources is a continuing curse. If it looms largest in the study of the archaic, more or less preliterary, periods of Greek and Roman history, that is only because those are the periods for which archaeological evidence is currently dominating the learned discussions. In fact, the lack of primary literary sources bedevils Greek history altogether after the death of Xenophon in the mid-fourth century BC, the whole of the history of the Hellenistic East, important periods of the history of the Roman Republic and of the Principate, including most of the history of the Roman provinces. For example, for the long reign of Augustus the only primary sources, other than documents, are half a book of the naive, superficial history by

Velleius Paterculus, some letters and speeches of Cicero for the early years, Augustus' own account of his stewardship, the *Res gestae*, a model of disingenuousness, and the Augustan poets. The only systematic account that survives is that of Dio Cassius, written near the middle of the third century. Dio used primary sources, to be sure, but our unavoidable reliance on his version is obviously unsatisfactory, as is the dependence on Virgil and Horace for much of the ideology of Augustus and his friends and supporters.

Nor is the situation significantly altered by introducing into the discussion written documents. Numerous as they may seem to be, they constitute a random selection in both time and place, and they often lack a meaningful context. It is hard to exaggerate. I cannot think of an ancient city, region or 'country', or of an institution (with two related exceptions to which I shall return in a moment), of which it is possible to write a systematic history over a substantial period of time. Some individual incidents can be presented historically, perhaps even something of the scale of Caesar's conquest of Gaul, but nothing beyond that. That is the unhappy consequence of our shortage of primary *historical* sources. Unless something is captured in a more or less contemporary historical account, the narrative is lost for all time regardless of how many inscriptions or papyri may be discovered. It is enough to point to the history of Athens and the Athenian empire in the nearly fifty years between the Persian and Peloponnesian wars, a period rich in epigraphical evidence but one for which Thucydides chose not to write a systematic account. We cannot even date some of the battles that Thucydides obviously thought important.

The exceptions are on the one hand in the history of ideas, specifically in the history of philosophy and science, of rhetoric, poetry and historiography, and on the other hand in the history of art and technology. In the former the distinction between literary and documentary sources loses most of its significance; in the latter, the 'documentary sources' are the objects themselves. There are serious gaps, too well known to need enumeration, and there are other difficulties, arising for instance from our uncertainty about the adequacy of the surviving samples; yet reasonable histories have been written of those subjects. Otherwise, the lack of primary sources for long stretches of time and for most regions of the Mediterranean creates a block not only for a narrative but also for the analysis of institutions. There are periods and places about which we have considerable knowledge, not only of the institutions but also of the detailed narrative of political history, of war and diplomacy, of the process of government, and so on – Athens in the latter part of the fifth century and much of the fourth century BC, the last century of the Roman Republic and the first two centuries of the Empire. However, this happy situation should not blind us to the inadequacy, often to the hopelessness, of the available evidence for the rest of Greece outside Athens, for the Roman Republic before the Gracchi, for most of the Roman provinces most of the time. Even for political history in the periods we know most about there are bad gaps, as I was compelled to confess repeatedly in my *Politics in the Ancient World*: it is enough to mention our fundamental ignorance of the way the *comitia tributa* worked, and that was the main legislative organ of the Roman Republic from early in the third century BC and the arena in which the tribunes operated. A complicating factor that reinforces the negative picture I am drawing is the random nature of the documentation that has come down to us, largely disconnected material detached from a larger context, illustrative but neither serial nor synoptic.

It is in the end not very surprising that university students of history, with some knowledge of the sources for, say, Tudor England or Louis XIV's France, find ancient history a 'funny kind of history'. The unavoidable reliance on the poems of Horace for Augustan ideology, or in the same way on the *Eumenides* of Aeschylus for the critical moment in Athenian history when the step was taken towards what we know as Periclean democracy, helps explain the appellative 'funny'. But the oddities are much more far-reaching, extending to the historians themselves in antiquity, in particular to two of their most pervasive characteristics, namely, the extensive direct quotation from speeches and the paucity of reference to (let alone quotation from) actual documents, public or private. The speeches are to us an extra-ordinary phenomenon and they produce extraordinary reactions among modern commentators. We have no good reason for taking the speeches to be anything but inventions by the historians, not only in their precise wording but also in their substance. Certainly that is how they were understood in antiquity: witness the discussion in his long essay on Thucydides (ch. 34–48) by Dionysius of Halicarnassus, the most acute and most learned of ancient critics and himself a prolific composer of speeches for his multi-volume *Roman Antiquities*.

Modern writers find themselves in difficulties. Not only does the position of a Dionysius of Halicarnassus seem immoral – it has been said that one would have to regard Thucydides as 'blind or dishonest'[11] – but, worse still, one must consider seriously abandoning some of the most interesting and seductive sections of Herodotus, Thucydides, Polybius, Caesar, Sallust, Livy, Tacitus, Dio Cassius and the rest as primary or secondary sources. There is no choice: if the substance of the speeches or even the wording is not authentic, then one may not legitimately recount that Pericles told the assembled Athenians in 430 BC that their empire 'is like a tyranny, seemingly unjust to have taken but dangerous to let go' (Thucydides 2.63.2). I have no idea what Pericles said on that occasion but neither have the innumerable historians who repeat from a speech what I have just quoted. Except for Thucydides and perhaps Polybius, there is no longer any serious argument, though the reluctance to accept the consequences is evident on all sides, if not always with such extreme gyrations as the 'demonstration' that Thucydides could have obtained precise, authentic information for all his speeches and even for the Melian Dialogue,[12] or the discovery that there are 'two kinds of veracity, the one of circumstance, the other of outlook and attitude'.[13]

I do not believe that it is possible to 'save' even Thucydides once it is held that the issue is one of honesty, of morality, in twentieth-century terms. After all, there can be no doubt that on innumerable occasions Thucydides reported as a simple matter of fact that a political figure, a military commander, even a group of people adopted a particular course of action as the consequence of a particular idea, opinion or judgment when that was at best the historian's own assessment of the reason for the action, an inference back from the act to the thought.[14] One striking form of several that he adopted was this: 'After making this speech Brasidas began to lead his army off, and the barbarians, seeing this, came on, shouting loudly and making a great din, thinking that he was running away and that they would catch him up and destroy him' (4.127.1). Are we to believe that Thucydides was conscious of cheating when he wrote such sentences innumerable times, or when he wrote all his speeches in his own style, when he had speakers reply to other speeches that they could not possibly have known about, when he invented the Melian Dialogue?[15]

It is an endlessly repeated commonplace that the speeches in the ancient historians represent a 'long-established convention' that 'recalls the long association of historiography from its earliest beginnings with epic and drama'.[16] No doubt, but no convention is unalterable, and if this one survived for a thousand years or more, it is untenable that every single practitioner was indifferent to the fact that he was a falsifier, the more blatantly so the more he insisted, with Thucydides and Polybius, that a historian was obligated to tell only the truth. Thucydides must have had something more in mind than just crude deception of his readers when, in the short statement of method in his first book, he wrote the awful part-sentence (1.22.1) that has exercised commentators for perhaps two centuries, with no prospect of a resolution of the difficulties: my method 'has been, while keeping as closely as possible to the general sense of the words that were actually said, to have the speakers say what, in my view, was called for by each situation'. We start from the wrong premise by assuming that Greeks and Romans looked upon the study and writing of history essentially as we do.[17] Collingwood suggested an alternative premise when he wrote in an anguished page on the speeches in Thucydides:

'Custom has dulled our susceptibilities; but let us ask ourselves for a moment: could a just man who had a really historical mind have permitted himself the use of such a convention? . . . Is it not clear that the style betrays a lack of interest in the question what such and such a man really said on such and such an occasion? . . . The speeches seem to me to be not history but Thucydidean comments upon the acts of the speakers, Thucydidean reconstructions of their motives and intentions . . ., a convention characteristic of an author whose mind cannot be fully concentrated on the events themselves, but is constantly being drawn away from the events to some lesson that lurks behind them, some unchanging and eternal truth of which the events are, Platonically speaking, *paradeigmata* or *mimemata*.'[18]

It was also a not self-evident habit of the ancient historians rarely to paraphrase and even more rarely to quote a document.[19] Thucydides notoriously failed to make any reference to documents in his statement of method (1.22) or to make overt use of them on all but a small number of occasions, although in a context that was essentially irrelevant to his history he demonstrated what could be done to squeeze out evidence by logical inference from two brief inscriptions (6.55). Part of the explanation for the universal indifference of the Greek and Roman historians to documents lies in their paucity and in the rudimentary state of the archives.[20] Modern historians have constantly to remind themselves that the paperasserie with which they are surrounded has not always been a 'natural' product of human behaviour. In the long history of the Graeco-Roman world, massive documentation characterized only the peculiar society of Egypt and to a limited extent the imperial courts of the later Roman Empire.

Records and documents, record-keeping and archives are a function of the society which produces and preserves them, or which largely fails to do one or the other.[21] The psychology and the needs of the Ptolemaic bureaucracy in Egypt had little in common with those of classical Greece or Rome. In the generation after Aristotle had initiated the scholarly collection and publication of various public records, Craterus, a Macedonian disciple, published a corpus of Athenian decrees in perhaps nine books.[22] Book 2 brought his collection past the middle of the fifth century BC, thus indicating the scarcity of earlier documents he was able to find; and the infrequency of identifiable uses of his collection in later centuries (except for abstruse linguistic or geographical points) suggests the absence of much interest in what we should consider to be an invaluable tool for historical study. As for Rome, hardly more than a hundred publicly displayed laws, *senatus consulta*, imperial 'enactments' and magisterial edicts are today available from the whole of the territory under Roman rule down to Constantine.[23] And it was not until Caesar's first consulate in 59 BC that the *acta* of the Senate were recorded and made public (Suetonius, *Caesar* 20.1). Before that only the bare bones of the decisions, the *senatus consulta*, were committed to writing.

In short, the epoch-making invention of literacy was followed for centuries by the survival of a fundamentally oral non-literate society. Man can function reasonably well in a pre-industrial society with little or no use of the written word. So when men came to write the history of their world, Greek or Roman, they found great voids in the inherited information about the past, or, worse still, quantities of 'data' that included fiction and half-fiction jumbled with fact. That is what modern historians, unwilling for whatever reason to admit defeat, to acknowledge a void, seek to rescue under the positive label, tradition (or oral tradition).[24] Few anthropologists view the invariably oral traditions of the people they study with the faith shown by many ancient historians. The verbal transmittal over many generations of detailed information about past events or institutions that are no longer essential or even meaningful in contemporary life invariably entails considerable and irrecoverable losses of data, or conflation of data, manipulation and invention, sometimes without visible reason, often for reasons that are perfectly intelligible. With the passage of time, it becomes absolutely impossible to control anything that has been transmitted when there is nothing in writing against which to match statements about the past. Again we suspect the presence of the unexpressed view that the traditions of Greeks and Romans are somehow privileged, though no one has yet demonstrated a plausible mechanism for the oral transmission of accurate information over a period of centuries (e.g. from archaic Greece to Pausanias in the second century A D, or from the Rome of the kings to Livy and Dionysius of Halicarnassus in the late first century B C). After all, it was in an era of literacy that the Roman nobility successfully paraded fraudulent genealogies at the end of the Republic,[25] or that Tacitus, Suetonius, and Dio Cassius, all of whom had access to contemporary writing, confused the account of the great fire in Rome in A D 64 so effectively that no one has been able to unscramble it satisfactorily.[26]

It is true that what we call 'literary tradition is an inadequate label for a very complex conglomeration of data', including linguistic information and data about religious practices, law and political institutions, as well as the narrative of wars, conspiracies and diplomacy.[27] However, the narrative is the queen of the tradition: without it, much of the other data would be unintelligible. How, for example, are we to use for the history of early Rome the fact that there was a close affinity between Latin and several other Italic languages spoken in or near Latium? What does that tell us by itself about Romans and Volsci or Romans and Sabines without the clues supposedly embedded in the literary tradition? There is no guarantee that the tradition has not arisen precisely in order to explain a linguistic, religious or political datum; that, in other words, the tradition is not an etiological invention – the rape of the Sabine women, for example.

The situation is not fundamentally different with respect to early Roman law, despite the survival of substantial chunks of the fifth-century Twelve Tables in easily translatable classical Latin. What, for example, does the following simple sentence from the Twelve Tables mean: 'Patronus si clienti fraudem facerit, sacer esto?' If we had to answer solely from the Twelve Tables, we should have to say that we have no idea. But we have the literary tradition, which refers to clients, and the answer is that we still do not know but that we have several different and incompatible explanations, several centuries later, but they have no claim to credence because they too did not know and they were unable to differentiate the early clientship from the institution of their own day. Indeed, they saw no need for serious differentiation: the Romans, like the Greeks, were 'relentlessly modernizing' in their attempts to deal with their own archaic institutions and behaviour.[28]

And why not? Since they lacked a 'conceptual framework' for the understanding of such institutions or of long-range social change,[29] their historians could not make proper sense of data, including documents, which their antiquarians discovered; nor could they assess the reliability of the data. Even we, who have no shortage of concepts, and long experience with techniques of evaluation and interpretation, are in grave difficulties over those periods for which the evidence is largely derived from oral tradition, and for which the documents are extremely few and essentially unintelligible.[30] Some of the supposed data are patently fictitious, the political unification of Attica by Theseus or the foundation of Rome by Aeneas, for example, but we quickly run out of such easily identified fictions. For the great bulk of the narrative we are faced with the 'kernel of truth' *possibility*, and I am unaware of any stigmata that automatically distinguish fiction from fact. The narrative as given by Livy and Dionysius (to which we may add Plutarch's lives of Theseus, Lycurgus or Solon) 'has to be ruthlessly scrutinized for signs of anachronism or embellishment', writes Ogilvie.[31] However, in an earlier work Ogilvie had already been gloomily dubious about the prospect when he pointed out that 'the hunt for anachronisms or contemporary references' in Livy's own late-Republican sources for the earliest period 'is peculiarly hazardous and unprofitable since every Caesarian allusion turns out on inspection to be equally Marian or Sullan'.[32] The only hope is a careful and judicious use of explanatory models (to which we shall turn in chapters 4 and 5). Without a theoretically grounded conceptual scheme, the thin and unreliable evidence lends itself to manipulation in all directions, without any controls.[33]

It is now time to return to the subject with which I began, namely, the place of archaeological evidence within the total source-material available to the ancient historian today.[34] Archaeology appears to be in a turmoil. In an understandable reaction against the 'counterfeit history' produced by earlier generations of anthropologists and archaeologists, a powerful sector among prehistorians has for some two decades been calling for a sustained effort to establish archaeology 'as a discipline in its own right, concerned with archaeological data which it clusters in archaeological entities displaying certain archaeological processes and studied in terms of archaeological aims, concepts and procedures'.[35] The global claims of the 'new archaeology' have been contested both within the discipline itself and outside.[36] Nevertheless, no serious student can or does ignore the work of its disciples in prehistory or in Near Eastern history, but in classical archaeology the heritage of Winckelmann, with its mixture of treasure-hunting and antiquated art history, still retains a considerable following, in some quarters the dominant one, affecting and restricting archaeological work from the initial choice of excavation sites to the final analysis of the finds.[37] In 1973 the then Reader and now Lincoln Professor of Classical Archaeology in the University of Oxford began a review-article with these words: 'A confrontation between the new archaeology and classical Greece has yet to take place, and perhaps never will, since the classical archaeologist is bound to a full and informative literary background and to art history beside which the contributions of new techniques will never be of great moment, and before which the practitioners of the new techniques are usually helpless, except in the detection of forgeries.'[38]

Well, the classical archaeologists concerned with Roman Britain have nothing like a full or informative literary background or great art to bind them, and accordingly they have long concerned themselves with 'settlement archaeology' and similar aspects of the 'new archaeology' of the prehistorians, though in their own terms rather than as disciples of the latter. By the 1950s comparable studies were being pursued by such archaeologists in Italy as Frank Brown of the American Academy in Rome and John Ward-Perkins of the British School, to name only two leading English-speaking figures, while the native school of Bianchi Bandinelli were engaging in a full-scale attack on the position now represented by Boardman. Greek archaeology was admittedly behindhand, but is rapidly catching up.[39] In short, the turmoil and the polemic have reached classical archaeology, too, and the debate touches the study of antiquity at a vital point, the quality and usefulness of the sources (those that are decidedly not forgeries, I need hardly add).

Welcome and indeed essential as the current debate is, it seems to me to be partly misdirected. To begin with, I believe it to be false to speak of the relationship between history and archaeology. At issue are not two qualitatively distinct disciplines but two kinds of evidence about the past, two kinds of historical evidence.[40] There can thus be no question of the priority in general or of the superiority of one type of evidence over the other; it all depends in each case on the evidence available and on the particular questions to be answered.

There are contexts in which the two types of evidence have to be deployed together so closely that in a sense neither is of much use without the other. As examples I cite the recent work of the Finnish Institute on Roman brick-stamps, and of Garlan on the amphora-stamps of Thasos.[41] In neither instance does the work I have mentioned exemplify the 'archaeological aims, concepts and procedures' proclaimed by the 'new archaeology'. The Roman bricks and the amphoras as objects tell us little in themselves and provide insufficient grounds for choosing among possible historical explanations, while the symbols and abbreviated words inscribed on them are similarly ambiguous or inconclusive without careful quantitative analysis both of the inscribed data and of the site-finds.[42]

Admittedly this kind of symbiotic situation is exceptional. Most commonly the two types of evidence complement each other in one way or another. And sometimes they appear to be mutually inconsistent or in direct conflict. Then one or the other must give way, and that usually (*but not always*) means the literary evidence, provided one can be certain that both the texts and the archaeological objects have been understood correctly, not necessarily an easy or certain conclusion. Once it was discovered, for instance, that many amphoras of the type Baldacci III, related to Dressel 6, originated in Istria, identified by Pliny (*Natural History*

15.8) as a major oil-producing centre, it was assumed that they were containers for oil, especially since in his discussion of wines Pliny had grouped north Italian wines under the rubric *reliqua* (14.67). Yet it is now clear that Pliny was not being dismissive in a quantitative sense, and that the Baldacci III pottery carried wine, not oil.[43] On the other hand, the disappearance by Trajan's time of the Dressel 2–4 type, which had long been the standard Italian wine container, has led to the conclusion that Italian wine export came to a fairly abrupt end at that time. However, the repeated and circumstantial literary evidence, notably of Galen and Fronto, for the continued popularity in the late second century of the famous Falernian wine of Campania cannot be brushed aside; one must therefore conclude that a change in containers occurred in or before Trajan's time although we have not yet been able to identify the replacement for Dressel 2–4.[44] That is the explanation recently offered by André Tchernia, and, though there is so far no confirmation, there is some encouragement in the discovery (mostly still unpublished) for the first time, in the sea off Civitavecchia and off the coast of Tuscany, of large liquid containers, known as *dolia*, up to 1.65m in height and 0.82m in maximum diameter.[45]

For reasons that are rooted in our intellectual history, ancient historians are often seduced into two unexpressed propositions. The first is that statements in the literary or documentary sources are to be accepted unless they can be disproved (to the satisfaction of the individual historian). This proposition derives from the privileged position of Greek and Latin, and it is especially unacceptable for the early periods of both Greek and Roman history, where the archaeological evidence bulks so large (and daily grows proportionally still larger) and where the quantitatively far from inconsiderable literary tradition is particularly suspect.[46] The second proposition is that the most insistent historical question one can put to an archaeological find is, Does it support or falsify the literary tradition? That approach gives automatic priority to literary evidence, and, in the history of early Rome, for example, has led to optimistic claims of archaeological support for the literary tradition, resting on highly selective tests.

One can read everywhere that archaeology now 'confirms in the essential the testimony of the annalistic' tradition.[47] In a sophisticated variant, the argument is that so long as history was only a narrative (*événementiel*), the hypercritical view of the tradition quite properly won the day, but with the switch to more sociological history and new archaeological techniques, renewed study of the topography and building history of the city of Rome confirms the main institutional and chronological lines of the tradition over the longer time-span (*dans la longue durée*), given the notorious conservatism of the Romans.[48]

This leaves me puzzled. The tradition about early Rome is almost entirely a narrative, *histoire événementielle*, and it remains that even though some present-day historians and archaeologists have changed their interest. The confirmation that is now being claimed proves to be in fact extremely restricted. That ancient buildings in the Forum can now be identified on the ground is an important discovery, but it is no confirmation of the traditional attribution of individual buildings to individual kings, an attribution which is too often chronologically impossible. Evidence is now available of the Aeneas myth and even of the Aeneas cult in central Italy as far back as the sixth century BC, but so far none of it from Rome itself.[49] Not surprisingly, therefore, the best modern accounts shift quickly from the question of Roman origins to the no less interesting, but wholly different, area of the intellectual and ideological history of the Roman Republic.[50] As for the relations in the 'regal period' between Rome and its neighbours, there is massive inconsistency between the literary account and what the archaeologists have unearthed.[51] It is sufficient to single out Satricum, a Latin settlement fifty kilometres south of Rome in an area of continuous conflict with the Volsci, mentioned for the first time by Dionysius of Halicarnassus (5.61.3) under date of 496 BC, though clearly by that time it had been one of the main centres in Latium for a century or more, with an important temple of the Italic Mater Matuta.[52]

Two decades of intensive inquiry into early Rome have culminated in the cul-de-sac of Satricum, suggesting that the ancient historian interested in evaluating his sources had better turn elsewhere. Let us instead consider the most numerous of all archaeological objects, of a kind that has been studied with particular care and sophistication in recent years, both on land and on wrecks in the sea – namely, pottery, the mostly un-adorned ceramic ware of daily use, containers, table and kitchen ware, cooking utensils, lamps; not the fine decorated ware that monopolized scholarly attention until recently, giving rise to the illusion that it somehow represented the major part of Graeco-Roman ceramic production. Plain utilitarian pottery can be, and was, made just about everywhere, literally in the millions each year, and fragments (sherds) turn up in vast numbers every year everywhere. Most of it was 'rigorously anonymous', especially the wares with the widest diffusion, from the Corinthian and bucchero pottery of the late archaic era through Attic black-glazed pottery and Campanian A, and on into the Roman im-perial age.[53] And the silence of the pots themselves is matched by almost total silence in the literary and epigraphical sources: 'Roman pottery is in a sense prehistoric'.[54] A better test of the mutual deployment and the limits of the two kinds of evidence can hardly be imagined.

The volume of publication in the past three decades on Roman pottery – with which I shall be exclusively concerned – has become almost unmanageable,[55] with particular attention to typology and chronology, the bases for all systematic study, and to the technological and economic aspects. Much has been learned; that the bulk of distribution was local; that shipment over longer distances was predominantly by water (the sea or navigable rivers); that the large containers, amphoras, were shaped for stowing in large ships and were the determining cargo in the selection of routes and ports of call; that other ceramic goods – table ware, cooking vessels, lamps – also shipped in large quantities, were 'parasitic' on the containers and their contents in their occupation of shipping space; and so on. Apart from the evidence provided by pottery marks of the practice of carrying the goods of a number of owners or merchants on a single vessel, most of the rest of what we know comes from the objects themselves, unaided by written texts in any form.

But so far there has been a major failure. In discussing the unparalleled diffusion throughout the Mediterranean basin of North African ceramic ware of every type, beginning about the middle of the second century A D and continuing with increased momentum virtually to the end of antiquity, a phenomenon not even mentioned in the surviving literature, Carandini has recently written: 'But we have not yet succeeded (for the moment) in extracting from these same products the most precious secret – the "social mode" in which they were produced.'[56] Apart from the optimistic 'for the moment', this judgment is shared by all the best students of Roman pottery, whether Italian, Gallic or North African.[57]

To begin with, not many kiln-sites have been identified, even fewer systematically investigated.[58] Secondly, the ownership of potteries and their labour force are unknown except for the relatively small number of cases in which amphora-marks indicate the presence or absence of slaves among the work-force. Our ignorance in this respect includes such central aspects as the relationship of the potters and potteries to the ownership of the land (including the clay-beds), to the men involved in the trade, or to 'branches' in other places. The possibilities are numerous and intricate, more so, I believe, than the speculations in the current literature allow for. That is decisively demonstrated by the publication in 1981 of three mid-third-century A D papyri from Oxyrhynchus.[59] They are contracts for two-year leases of the potteries on large estates (the phrase used in the text) in the district, where the tenants, who identify themselves as 'potters who make wine jars', undertake to produce per annum respectively 15,000, 24,000 and 16,000 jars of a capacity of four choes, for which they are to be paid 32 drachmas per 100 in the first two cases, but 36 per 100 in the third. They are also to manufacture a small number of two- and eight-choes jars, to be paid for in jars of wine or amounts of lentils. The landlords are to provide the potteries, the equipment and the raw materials, the potters only the labour-force (unspecified). And in two of the cases (the unpublished ones) other evidence reinforces the view that the landowners were people of considerable substance.[60]

To the best of my knowledge, this possibility has been ignored in the speculations about the status of potters and potteries. I do not suggest that the Oxyrhynchus leases represent a common method of putting potteries into production in the Roman world (though I see no way to demonstrate that it was uncommon). I merely wish to make the simple point that archaeological evidence or archaeological analysis *by itself* cannot possibly uncover the legal or economic structure revealed by the Oxyrhynchus papyri or the alternative structures in Arezzo, Puteoli, Lezoux or North Africa. The burst of polemical rhetoric with which Carandini closes his survey of the history of North African ware in the final centuries of antiquity[61] serves only to divert attention from the absence of data about the 'social mode of production' of that ware, and, in my view, the impossibility of ever overcoming that gap in our knowledge from archaeological evidence alone. Not for the first time in my life, I quote Stuart Piggott:

'Technology is something that can be illuminated by direct archaeological evidence . . . and from that . . . we can move towards inferring something of subsistence-economics and of man as part of his ecological surroundings. But when we try to infer such things as social structure or in the broadest sense religious practices, such evidence becomes almost wholly ambiguous.'[62]

This 'hard doctrine', as Piggott once referred to it rather tongue-in-cheek,[63] remains unacceptable to those who are prepared to call Troy II 'urban' (or at least 'proto-urban') in the Early Bronze Age, when its area was only about two acres.[64] 'It is simply a question of definition of terms,' writes Renfrew, and, directly inspired by this savagely reductionist view, Guidi has now dated the proto-urban phase of Rome back to the end of the ninth century BC.[65] That such a typology is of much use to an historian is doubtful: the critical definition of terms is not something to be achieved so 'simply'.[66] The study of amphoras is today primarily a study of production and trade, and the evidence which amphoras provide, it has recently been concluded, 'can only be properly assessed against the background of what we know about the system of marketing from literature, epigraphy, and the still under-utilized legal sources'.[67] I should qualify that: I see no reason for distinguishing the 'evidence' of the amphoras and the 'background of what we know' from other kinds of sources. What ties them all together in the end is the conceptual framework from which the historian works, a framework which, we saw earlier, the historians in antiquity lacked for the inquiry we are now concerned with; and which historians today possess in super-abundance.

[3]

Documents[1]

In opening his London Inaugural Lecture, entitled 'Ancient Economic History', A. H. M. Jones wrote as follows: 'The chief problem of ancient economic history is one that I hesitate to confess before a mixed audience . . . lest ancient history should be brought into disrepute. However, it is unlikely that I shall long be able to conceal the ignominious truth, that there are no ancient statistics.'[2] He went on, after exemplifying the situation, to conclude that 'it is not very profitable to attack the economic problems of the ancient world from a statistical angle. Some limited results can be achieved, and have been achieved, in a few fields, . . . but more ambitious projects cannot but become a frail tissue of tenuous conjectures.'

The tone of that programmatic statement is as important as its substance. It was written in 1948, on the threshold of the explosive impact of econometrics on historians and the rapid emergence of the new quantitative history (or serial history or cliometrics). But what Jones meant by 'statistics' had nothing to do with correlations, regression analysis, standard deviations, scaling methods, factor analysis; the term meant little more than presenting numbers in the form of tables or graphs, calculating averages and noting minima and maxima. Thus, money seems to have been worth five times less in Demosthenes' day than in Solon's two centuries earlier; there were more than 10,000 private houses within the walls of Athens, ranging in price from 300 to 12,000 drachmas; the normal charge for a prostitute ranged from a half-obol to two drachmas (twelve half-obols), though a Laïs could get 10,000 drachmas for one night. These examples have been taken at random from Book I of the first edition (1817) of August Boeckh's 1000-page *Die Staatshaushaltung der Athener*. There is no shortage of numbers in the ancient sources – they may run to a million – and no shortage of antiquarians and historians who have collected them, manipulated them and drawn wide-ranging conclusions from them in the past two centuries. Jones knew that, and yet he was not wrong to conclude that 'there are no ancient statistics', that 'more ambitious projects' to fabricate statistics (my verb, not his) 'cannot but become a frail tissue of tenuous conjectures'. He came to that conclusion from the notorious unreliability of so many of the figures, from their selection according to purposes that gave strong preference to untypical quantities, from the difficulty (if not impossibility) of grouping the innumerable isolated data into meaningful combinations, whether within a given period or over longer time-scales.

Yet the passion for numbers in ancient history, strongest in demographic and economic history but increasingly common in other branches as well, has increased since Boeckh's day. One understands the psychology. Numbers give an appearance of 'objectivity', of 'science', which is in fact not warranted without a great deal of justification in each instance, and they make the historian's account more vivid, more 'real' to the reader. 'Twelve' seems to tell much more than 'very rarely', though as an isolated number it may be wrong and is anyway less meaningful. So deep-grained is this psychology, coupled with the ancient historian's feeling of inferiority towards his fortunate colleagues in modern or even medieval history (Jones's 'ignominious truth'), that many are unable to resist weaving a 'frail tissue of tenuous conjectures'. Jones himself was a confirmed non-resister. I give one example: in a short general article on ancient slavery he calculated that a slave in the Roman empire in the second century A D 'cost eight to ten times his annual keep as against a year or a year and a quarter's annual keep' in fourth-century B C Athens.[3] I shall not repeat the fantastic arithmetic by which the price for a 'normal slave' and the cost to his owner of his maintenance were arrived at, by manipulating a handful of miscellaneous literary references from heterogeneous contexts, most of which were obviously meant to be humorous or absurd, such as the short satirical poem by Martial (6.66) about an auction of a prostitute during which the auctioneer kissed the lady several times 'in order to demonstrate her purity', whereupon the man who bid 600 sesterces withdrew his bid. I cite this particular effort not because I propose to spend time demonstrating the pointlessness of such arithmetic, but for two other reasons: the first is to note the widespread prior fallacy, that any two comparisons are *ipso facto* meaningful, in this case between one Greek city in the fourth century B C and the whole of the Roman Empire as a single unity five hundred years later;[4] secondly, because of the magnetism of such calculations (strengthened by a touch of caution: 'eight to ten times'), among specialists who commonly repeat the conclusions without checking what lies behind them, and among non-specialists who accept them on the *auctoritas* of the original author.[5]

I hasten to add that Jones was one of the most authoritative ancient historians of our time and one of the most intelligent and skilful manipulators of the numbers found in ancient texts. That is precisely what makes this example a significant and not unfair one. I hasten to add, too, that I welcome all legitimate efforts to quantify data in ancient history, as I welcome the new serial history – welcome and envy – though I stop well short of Furet's sharp dichotomy, a 'problem-history (*histoire-problème*) in place of a narrative history'.[6]

There is a sense in which it is right to insist that what has been called the 'statistical epoch' did not begin until some time in the nineteenth century, that everything that went before was a 'pre-statistical epoch',[7] but there is another, perhaps more important sense, in which the most fundamental divide came much earlier, somewhere not too late in the Middle Ages. Thus, several decades ago the question was posed 'whether a critical examination of taxation data can be made to yield any conclusion as to broad changes in the geographical distribution of wealth' in England.[8] A first study covered the long span from 1086 to 1843, a second examined only the period 1334–1649. Both employed two advanced statistical methods, Spearman's rank-order correlation and Pearson's product moment correlation coefficient, and came to different conclusions (each presented in statistical detail), not because either made mathematical mistakes or overlooked essential documentation, but because of different assessments of the biases in the data and of the weighting of certain variables.[9]

I mention the disagreement only in passing, in order to illustrate the point that even the best work in modern serial history cannot escape the limitations and risks inherent in complex multivariate analysis which requires holding some variables steady, marshalling others, and assuming the magnitude and behaviour of still others: the result will be, or at least always has been so far, sharp disagreement and controversy, not over the techniques as such but over the analytical choices and the resulting conclusions. But the chief reason that I gave this particular example is to support my statement that the first unbridgeable divide came between ancient and (at least later) medieval history. An ancient historian can easily enough *ask* a comparable question; for example, what was the geographical distribution of wealth among the provinces of the Roman empire and how did it change between Augustus and Diocletian? Even omitting the second half of the question, he cannot proceed to the indispensable next question, which tax data (or any comparable data) can be made to yield an answer? There are no such data. The best he can offer, at times with considerable plausibility, is such an answer as 'Pannonia was poorer (or even much poorer) than Gaul'.

'The principal cause of our ignorance', Jones explained in his Inaugural Lecture, 'is that the bulk of our evidence . . . is literary and not documentary.' The literary evidence is vitiated by massive corruption in the manuscript tradition and initially by the indifference of most ancient writers to economic matters as well as by their casualness and carelessness in giving numbers; the available documentary evidence consists overwhelmingly of the papyri from Egypt, 'a fortuitous agglomeration of documents and scraps of documents mainly of ephemeral importance', mostly 'in a highly fragmented state' and 'extremely parochial' (all the more so since there are virtually none from Alexandria where soil conditions are unsuitable for the preservation of discarded papyrus). No ancient historian would disagree, but if that were the whole explanation, we should be forced to the conclusion that the ancient historian is in his uniquely handicapped situation only because of bad luck: his tax records have failed to survive, the medievalist's luckily have survived in sufficient number. 'If' (to quote Jones once more) 'we possessed the merest fraction of the statistical material compiled by ancient governments, we should have little cause to complain.'

There is nothing to do about Lady Luck but grumble, an unprofitable exercise. I suggest that something more fundamental is involved, that even if we did have a respectable fraction of government-compiled figures our position would be as disreputable as it is in their absence. A number is a number is a number may be good Gertrude Stein, but it is a false though commonly assumed equation in historical analysis or comparison especially over time. The collection and computation of numbers, of statistics, as well as the keeping of records more generally are a function of the particular society in which that kind of activity is carried on, and the function changes, often radically, as the society changes. That is the proposition I propose to examine, concentrating on the ancient *written documents* while calling on the literary material from time to time for corroboration or elucidation. In a sense, all original documents that have survived from antiquity are available because of archaeological activity, professional or amateur, deliberate or accidental. If I restrict myself to those documents that have writing on them (or a symbolic equivalent), even if no more than a stamp on a brick or tile, that is not because I denigrate the growing importance of 'silent' archaeological data but solely because the methods and problems of their evaluation and interpretation require somewhat different considerations and a proper inquiry would outrun my space limits.

Two preliminary distinctions have to be made, both fairly obvious. The first is between documents emanating from and directed to private individuals (or groups such as a tax-farming association) and those issued by a public body, either the state, a subdivision of the state (such as an Athenian deme) or a temple. The second rests on whether a document was intended for private circulation or for public notice. It is only a minor complication that some categories of documents cannot be neatly pigeonholed: a private letter from a Roman emperor, for example, was likely to be displayed by the recipient, in the case of a city even on a stone or bronze tablet. Such 'hybrids' need not detain us. What is important, indeed sobering, to appreciate is the small number of categories that dominate the surviving material numerically. Running into the hundreds of thousands are brick- and pottery-stamps, inscribed grave-stones, coin legends and symbols, and the papyri from Graeco-Roman Egypt. The latter range from receipts and brief memoranda to letters, tax-lists or copies of royal decrees, all surviving because of the peculiar ecology south of the Delta in a unique region that depended entirely on river irrigation. After that, the totals for each type of document drop to tens of thousands and often to thousands – for the whole of Graeco-Roman antiquity, a thousand years or so over much of Europe, northern Africa and western Asia, one must always remember.[10]

The first question to be asked about any document is about the reason or motive for its having been written. That question is not asked often enough, because it is unconsciously assumed that motives and purposes are self-evident, that is to say, that they are more or less the same as our own. On the contrary, I would argue that in antiquity the purpose of all documents was either to communicate some information (or misinformation) or to memorialize something, but not to provide data for policy-making or for analysis, past, present or future.

In his brief but detailed account of the duties of Athenian officials in his day, Aristotle described how certain financial records were kept in order to allow for the fact that different payments fell due in different periods (prytanies) of the year, some in instalments spread up to ten years. 'As for the taxes farmed out for one year,' he wrote (*Constitution of Athens* 47.2–48.1), the *poletai* 'inscribe the name of the "buyer" and the amount on whitewashed tablets and turn them over to the Council. In addition they inscribe on ten tablets those who must make payments in each prytany; a tablet for each payment for those who must pay three times a year; another for those who pay in the ninth prytany . . . The tablets are therefore brought to the Council inscribed according to the (due dates of the) payments; they are guarded by the public slave.' When a payment fell due, the financial officials (*apodektai*) 'erased the payments made, in the presence of the Council in the Council-chamber, and returned the tablets to the public slave.'

These tablets will have been abstracted from the original records of the sales and leases for which the *poletai* were responsible (taxes farmed out, state properties, mines, confiscated properties). Anyone who wished to examine the situation would have had to consult both the lists of original transactions, wherever they were stored, and the lists of future payers, that is, those whose names had not been eradicated on the white-washed boards held in custody by a single public slave. Only two purposes could have been served by such a clumsy form of documentation: details on monies still owing to the state and a check on crude official malfeasance. The inadequacy of the documentation may surprise us but it would have been self-evident in a society in which the official roster of citizens was also kept in a remarkably casual manner.[11]

Athens was not only the largest Greek city-state and the one likely to have been involved in the largest number of financial transactions, it was also the quintessentially democratic one with the most powerful reason to pursue what we may well call the 'police function' of documents and records. There is therefore no reason to assume (and no evidence to support the view) that other city-states kept records designed for more 'advanced' or complex uses. So few are available today that the proposition cannot be fully tested, but there is one essential pointer, namely, the failure to create a bureaucracy, without which continuous records and their combination for purposes of analysis and prognostication are literally impossible.

Only Graeco-Roman Egypt, conceivably the Seleucid empire (about which we know next to nothing on this aspect), and in a rudimentary way Rome under the emperors were sufficiently bureaucratic. What, if any, were the practical consequences? Unfortunately, as I have already mentioned, there are no papyri from Alexandria, so that the only public documents we have from the capital are those that were originals or copies in the possession of officials in the countryside. However, they are sufficiently numerous to reveal a paperasserie on a breathtaking scale and an equally stupendous illusion. Presumably such items as tax receipts and tax lists reflected actual payments and receipts with reasonable accuracy, but the policy documents and plans expressed the King Canute conception of power: the god-king commanded the waves to stand still, his subjects to plant every square metre precisely as he ordered, to dispose of the crop as he ordered, to buy and sell at his fixed prices. And the subjects responded as the waves of the sea. Recent research has demonstrated that, contrary to the view of earlier generations of papyrologists with their faith in an Egyptian 'planned economy', 'mercantilism', 'state capitalism', even 'state socialism', all this documentation is largely misleading in the study of economic history, valuable though it is for its insights into the mentality of the kings and their vast bureaucracy.[12] A bureaucracy may be a necessary condition for documentation suitable for economic analysis, it is not a sufficient condition.

The appetite for paper spread to private affairs: every payment, order, instruction, complaint or whatever was put into writing (on papyrus or on potsherds), in contrast to classical Greek practice. A Greek in Ptolemaic Egypt would have been both amused and bewildered by the necessity felt by the plaintiff in one Athenian lawsuit (Ps.–Demosthenes 49.5), who was seeking to recover four debts owing to his deceased father, the banker Pasion, to explain to the jury how he knew the precise total, 4438 drachmas and 2 obols. Bankers, he said, 'are accustomed to write memoranda of the monies they give out and the purpose, and of the sums which someone pays, so that the receipt and the payments may be known to them for their reckoning.' Anyone today who has spent an hour with Graeco-Roman papyri will fully appreciate the contrast.

One collection of such documents, conventionally known as the 'Zenon Papyri', is worth consideration in the present context.[13] More than two thousand have been published, dating from 261 BC to certainly 239 and possibly as late as 229, all from a single estate in the Fayum, an oasis reclaimed by the first Ptolemies. The 2800-hectare estate was a revocable 'gift' (*dorea*) from Ptolemy II Philadelphus to his chief financial officer Apollonius, farmed intensively for most of the period under the management of an Asia Minor Greek named Zenon. The papyri include a substantial number of official documents but a large majority are private papers of every conceivable variety. (Given the position of Apollonius and the character of Ptolemaic rule, the categories 'official' and 'private' are not easily distinguishable, but that is irrelevant for my purposes.) Zenon was a remarkable man, eagle-eyed, imaginative, audacious, adventurous, for whom no action was too small or too large for his personal attention. Yet modern scholars, after more than half a century of intense research, have not progressed beyond an enumeration of details about the enterprise. Here is a typical example:

'Let us rapidly review the various branches of pasturage . . . Some figures, even though incomplete, give an idea of the importance of the livestock of Philadelphia. For the royal feasts, 42 calves were sent by Apollonius to Alexandria. An enumeration of sheep reached the total of 6731. One shepherd was entrusted with 536 sheeps and 10 goats, another leased 144 goats. One tax account mentions 500, another 366. A herd of pigs counted 400 grown animals and 211 young; a report on the organization of the piggeries envisages that 70 animals would be entrusted to each of nine designated swineherds . . .

'As for the tenants who worked the land of the *dorea*, did they possess those necessary instruments of exploitation, pack-asses and plough-oxen? In one case, Zenon advanced to tenants the money with which to purchase an ass for the transport of their crops. There were others to whom the ass was loaned. But when it was necessary to bring in the harvest, it happened that instead of lending asses to the peasants, Zenon requisitioned animals from them. That provoked vociferous complaints . . .'[14]

Such an account covering all of Zenon's activities no doubt leaves a vivid impression, or rather a kaleidoscope, of his society, but to call it 'a synthesis of economic history'[15] is to strip the word 'synthesis' of its essential meaning. It is similarly fallacious to call the whole collection of the Zenon papyri 'the Zenon archive' (or 'dossier'), any more than the contents of my desk drawers can legitimately be called an archive. Jones's 'fortuitous agglomeration of documents and scraps of documents mainly of ephemeral importance' describes not only the papyri we happen to have recovered but, in my view, also the original collection. Mere chance, luck, has deprived us of the enumeration of all the animals on the estate that Apollonius once requested of Zenon,[16] and no doubt numbers of similar documents also existed. If the more than two thousand Zenon papyri that have been recovered from the debris and the incalculable number that have not been recovered were in fact all retained by Zenon and not thrown away, presumably he and his assistants could with considerable effort have produced more synthetic accounts, perhaps of the annual grain yield over the whole period of his management, of price fluctuations, of changes in the crop-mix, and so on.[17] However, all the evidence satisfies me that such notions were alien to him and his society, that his mass of paper consisted of day-to-day documents intended for day-to-day purposes and little more: instructions, purchase orders, payment orders, receipts in minute detail. And I believe the same to be true of the royal records. Because the psychology of the regime required obedience to royal instructions for every moment and every action in the lives of the subjects, the mass of paper gives the illusion of all-embracing retrospective accounting and forward planning, but it is only an illusion.

Available Roman documents are so scarce that they add nothing to what I have already said. However, the agricultural manuals of Cato, writing in the middle of the second century B C, and of Columella two centuries later are interesting. Cato was a cataloguer, not only of strictly agronomic details but of everything else, of the number of pots and pans required on a typical estate, of the clothing to be given out to the slaves at stated intervals, of the distribution of work assignments in summer and winter, *ad infinitum*. In contrast, all his economic judgments are unsupported assertions, from the initial decision on the selection of an estate, through his advice on crop selection to what he has to say about marketing. His well-known maxim, wherever possible, sell, don't buy, reveals complete innocence of the notion of cost-effectiveness, and Mickwitz demonstrated fifty years ago that Cato (and the others) in fact lacked the accounting techniques essential for even a rudimentary analysis.[18] Proof is provided by the 'more professional' Columella, who does try some calculations from which modern writers have derived figures for the average cost of farmland and average rates of profit that now recur in nearly all writing on Roman economic history, though it is demonstrable (and has in fact been demonstrated) that Columella's arithmetic cannot bear the weight that has been put upon it.[19]

I am not being naive. Of course, Cato or Columella or any attentive landowner, especially if he had a good and honest bailiff, had reasonable rule-of-thumb knowledge, from his own experience and that of others, whether in any given place at any given time on any given piece of land it was preferable to plant vines rather than cereals, and so on, even if he could not justify his decisions by cost accounting. Furthermore – and I consider this to be psychologically decisive – the rate of exploitation was so great that holders of larger estates in antiquity regularly derived considerable revenue from their holdings. They needed records only as a check on day-to-day operations and on the honesty and diligence of their staffs or their tenants (a police function again). Smallholders had no options and therefore no need for paper except as possible protection against illegal exploitation.

Outside Egypt, governmental documents available to us are solely those that the authorities chose to display publicly in lasting materials, stone or bronze (apart from the quotations that are preserved in the literary sources). The question of motive is then critical, and the first and most obvious point is that the procedure is intimately bound up with the nature of the political system. For the centuries before Alexander the Great, Athens was unique among the Greek city-states, 'publishing' a remarkable variety of documents – the survivors now number in the thousands – whereas Corinth, for example, has produced virtually none, the Greek cities of Sicily only a handful. That the contrast is nothing more than the result of archaeological accident can no longer be maintained: classical Corinth, for example, has been thoroughly excavated down to virgin soil. It must follow that we have a reflection of Athenian democracy on the one hand, of Corinthian (and other) oligarchy on the other hand. I say 'Athenian' because none of the other Greek democracies followed Athenian practice; that is an interesting distinction that requires further investigation.

For many centuries after Alexander, other variations developed but there is no need to enumerate them, though it is worth noting that of all the publicly displayed Roman laws, *senatus consulta* and imperial 'enactments' down to Constantine, barely one hundred are now available in some condition from the whole of the territory under Roman rule. For the whole of antiquity, in sum, what we have at our disposal (apart from Athens) is a scatter of documents from one end of the Mediterranean world to the other, the great majority of them isolated texts without a context, hence not only without a good basis for interpretation (let alone comparison or generalization) but also without a basis for understanding why this particular document was made public and not an indeterminate number of others.[20] Two illustrations will suffice.

1 – Shortly before his death, Alexander ordered the Greek cities to recall all their exiles, an order he had proclaimed by the herald at the Olympic Games of 324 BC. We need not believe the story that more than 20,000 exiles had assembled at Olympia to greet the announcement, but there can be no doubt that the continuous civil strife had created exiles in the tens of thousands. Not all were willing or able to return home, but there were enough of them to create terrible complications. The literary sources merely hint at the political and social difficulties, but they are silent about the no less complex property complications. Exile was regularly accompanied by confiscation of property, which was redistributed in one way or another to members of the victorious faction. Restoration of the exiles without some measure, at least, of restoration of their property would have reduced Alexander's decree to an

empty gesture. What was done? Two inscriptions, one from the city of Mytilene on the island of Lesbos, the other from Tegea on the mainland of Greece (posted at Delphi), record the steps taken in those two communities. Unfortunately, both stones are now incomplete, the one from Tegea so fragmentary that much of the restoration by editors is often no more than guesswork, and to a considerable extent they are hardly intelligible. But this much is clear, that the situation was almost too difficult to be dealt with, and that the two cities tried different approaches. Little of significance emerges beyond that, though it is obvious that if we had full details from a sufficient number of cities, we should know more about property in fourth-century Greece outside Athens, particularly about the law of property, than we know today from all the available sources together, literary as well as epigraphical. As they stand, however, little that has been written on the basis of these two isolated texts is either significant or trustworthy.[21]

2 – An unusually long and legible inscription from Ephesus publicized the detailed rules for debt-relief necessitated by a war that had devastated the countryside and created a crisis. As the beginning and the end of the inscription are missing, there is no date, and there is nothing in the text itself to indicate which war caused the trouble, in an area that experienced more than one damaging invasion. For reasons we need not examine, nineteenth-century scholars opted for a relatively late date, most of them for the Mithridatic War in the 80s BC; by a circular argument the text was then cited as evidence of the scale and consequences of that war and also of the changes that had occurred from earlier times in the rules regarding loans secured by property. In 1912 an expert on the Ephesian inscriptions produced unanswerable palaeographical arguments for a date early in the third century BC, and so the struggle among Alexander's successors for Asia Minor replaced the Mithridatic War.[22] The text provides confirmation that the wars of the successors were savage and destructive, a fact already well enough known, and it gives us welcome new information about the rules of hypothecation outside Athens, tantalizing information, however, as can be seen in the lack of agreement among legal historians.

And not much else: for example, we are left guessing about the reason for the considerable amount of borrowing on landed property even before the war, or for the apparent lack of serious concern with questions of urban debts.

The documents we have just been considering arose in grave emergencies and it is easy to appreciate why it was necessary to give them full publicity. Given the nature of communication in this world, that could be accomplished only by posting in the town square or some other central place. It is less obvious, however, why the posting should have been on stone, with its promise of permanence, a promise that tends to become a reality to the modern historian when he reads the same stones two thousands years later. For how many years, one wonders, did the Ephesians find it necessary or possible to leave the stone recording debt regulations standing? Sheer overcrowding of the available spaces must have determined the answer in many cases. Some of the Athenian stones that we now read have survived precisely because they were taken down for such new, mundane uses as paving-blocks or the lining of wells. But, as we shall see in a moment, others survived *in situ* for centuries without any apparent justification.

If we concentrate on the many Athenian inscriptions relating to public finance, it is obvious, given the habit of posting on stone, why the practice should have embraced lists of tribute payments from the 'allies' during the empire or the proceeds from the sale at auction of property confiscated from the men found guilty in 415 BC of the mutilation of the herms and the profanation of the Eleusinian mysteries. The political significance of such publicity needs no discussion. It is perhaps less obvious why the sums paid out of the treasury for a particular military campaign should be similarly recorded in perpetuity, or, in the fourth century BC, the full catalogue of warships and their equipment or the annual leasing of concessions in the silver mines, each carefully defined by boundary indications.

The extreme attention to detail is best exemplified by the stelae recording the sales of the confiscated property following the double impiety of 415. A large number of fragments have been found with more than one thousand lines of text, mostly in the area of the Eleusinion in the southeastern corner of the Agora, and it has been calculated that originally they were parts of ten (or possibly eleven) stelae.[23] Slightly more than one quarter of the names known to have been denounced (Andocides 1.12–18) appear, so that the full, impressive stone display may have been still larger. The enormous length of the document was necessitated by the fact that every single item sold by the *poletai* was listed separately along with its price and the sales tax (roughly one per cent), ranging from a pallet and a brazier, each sold for two obols, to a group of scattered estates in Euboea, belonging to the otherwise unknown Oionias, that brought in $81\frac{1}{3}$ talents, four times the hitherto largest known holding in Attica, that of the banker Pasion (Ps.–Demosthenes 46.13), unless the stone-cutter had made a mistake in copying.

Although one can appreciate that Athenians derived pleasure and satisfaction from reading the amounts of tribute paid by each subject-state, it strains the imagination excessively to think that they were equally interested in knowing one by one the value of every piece of pottery, utensil and implement confiscated from Alcibiades, or the nationality and price of each of the sixteen slaves of Cephisodotus the metic. The task of collecting the data without a proper bureaucracy was a considerable one – eighteen months is a fair estimate of the time required.[24] Lists were necessary for the auctions, held at intervals, but why were the permanent complete lists inscribed and placed on public display when the sales were completed? The explanation must be sought in what I have earlier called the 'police function' of ancient financial documents and records,[25] though at least three difficulties with that explanation should be noticed.

It is decisive that among the many Athenian financial inscriptions, there is no trace of a synoptic text, for example, one summarizing the annual income or expenditure of the Athenian state.[26] Apart from legislative documents or inter-state agreements, every text we have reports on the activities of specific officials, in such detail that anyone who wished could check the accounts down to one-obol transactions and, if necessary, bring an accusation of malfeasance. However, the first difficulty with this group of stelae is, as Lewis saw, that 'attempts to add up figures are sporadic and inefficient. There are variations even in these additions, depending on how the sales-taxes are dealt with.'[27] Secondly, land and houses bought from the *poletai* could be paid for over ten and five years, respectively, and the payments (or defaults) were recorded not on the original lists but on the annual white-washed tablets already discussed, without which no proper check on the officials was possible. Finally, there is the mystery of the lifetime of these stelae: they were still standing near the Eleusinion in the time of Eratosthenes (d. 194 BC) and possibly even in Byzantine times.[28] Why? They could have retained neither a police nor an analytical function for more than a few years, and it is no less difficult to attribute a memorial function to them. When Alcibiades returned from exile in 407 BC to assume supreme command of the Athenian war effort, the assembly voted not only to annul the sentence of death and confiscation and to revoke the priestly curses against him but also to cast into the sea the tablets recording his fate (Diodorus 13.69.2 et al.). I have no suggestion as to why the stelae of the *poletai* were not similarly removed, or why they were left standing for two centuries and possibly many more.

That is but one of a complex of questions with ramifications extending beyond economic history to the life of the *polis* as a whole. Beginning almost certainly in the year 367/6 BC, the Athenian *poletai* annually inscribed on marble stelae set up in the Agora the full details of the concessions in the silver mines that it was their duty to lease out.[29] This practice was continued into the next century and presumably ceased when the democracy was finally abolished in 261 BC. But why did they not begin earlier, given that they had been 'publishing' records of other activities for at least half a century and had been leasing mining rights even earlier? We have no clue. A different kind of question is raised by the fragments of stelae recording the dedication to Athena by (or on behalf of) freed slaves of silver bowls weighing one hundred drachmas each.[30] The occasion for the dedication was the 'victory' of the freedman in a fictitious lawsuit against his or her ex-owner, one of the peculiar devices for manumission known from the Greek world. More than three hundred individuals appear in the surviving fragments, to be dated on palaeographical and onomastic grounds to the years immediately following 330 BC. This particular device is otherwise unknown, and that suggests that it was an abnormal one employed only during this short period. Presumably peculiar conditions had arisen in Athens to provoke both its introduction and its rapid abandonment, and again we have no clue.

It would help if we knew something about public archives, but we know virtually nothing except that much documentation was never filed there at all, and that the archives tended to become fuller from the fourth century BC on.[31] That has been demonstrated for the Greek world generally and I see little reason to think that the same was not true of Athens. It follows, I believe, from this and from the restricted range of documents that we possess, that the failure of our literary sources to give figures can be attributed as much to their ignorance as to their indifference. The very possibility of ignorance hardly enters the endless modern discussion of dubious figures; it is drowned out by learned consideration of manuscripts, palaeography, textual emendation.[32] When a second-century AD compiler attributes to Aristotle the figure of 470,000 slaves for Aegina (Athenaeus 6.272c) – a figure few have the foolhardiness to defend, given that the total area of the island is 80 km^2 – no one seems to ask himself, how did Aristotle know that or any other slave-population total? Who counted, and where was the count recorded? Is it not at least a worry that in the very large corpus of Aristotle's surviving works there is not a single comparable figure, not even in the *Constitution of Athens*? Or, on what documentation did Thucydides conclude (8.40.2) that there were more slaves in Chios than in any other *polis* save Sparta? The Athenian slaves, according to another figure given by Athenaeus, allegedly from a census taken late in the fourth century BC by Demetrius of Phalerum, totalled four hundred thousand. Did Chios have more? Was Thucydides wrong? Or Athenaeus? The study of ancient economic history is not advanced by the incessant playing about with a handful of such ungrounded numbers.

I do not counsel despair. What I seek is a shift in the still predominant concentration of research from individual, usually isolated documents to those that can be subjected to analysis collectively, and where possible in a series over time; an emancipation from the magnetism of the words in an individual text in favour of a quasi- (or even pseudo-) statistical study. I give two examples, each of groups of documents that individually supply no more information than, say, a modern railway ticket or sales invoice.

1 – In the period roughly between 400 and 250 BC, the Athenians adopted a simple device for giving public notice that a piece of property was legally encumbered: they inscribed a slab of stone with a few words and placed it as a marker on a farm or in the wall of a house. When I completed my inquiry into these documents in 1951, the texts of 222 had been published, 182 of them in a sufficiently complete state to be analysed. The texts ran from three to fifteen words and a numeral or two (indicating a sum of money), and yet I was able to demonstrate that these stones marked indebtedness on the part of wealthier Athenian landowners, almost always for such conventional personal expenses as dowries; that, in other words, they are not evidence for a steady decline in the Athenian peasantry in the fourth century BC, the interpretation that was generally accepted by generations of historians on the *sole testimony of these stones falsely interpreted*.[33]

2 – In July 1875 there was found in a house in Pompeii a wooden box containing heavily carbonized, waxed wooden tablets, 12–15 cm by 10–12 cm in size. In the end, 153 more or less legible documents were reconstituted from the find, perhaps ten of them diptyches, the rest triptyches, all witnessed receipts for payments by the *argentarius* L. Caecilius Iucundus, a few to a public slave of Pompeii for a lease of something from the city, the great majority for payments made on behalf of unnamed buyers to the vendors of objects sold at auction.[34] The collection is so far unique: it is 'the only document of archives in the Latin language discovered to this day that concerns the Roman bank'[35] (with the important qualification that the 'archive' consists of a very small

selection made for reasons that escape us), and it has made possible a view of the place of a 'banker' in the economy and society of a provincial Italian city (in particular of the men with whom he associated in his affairs) far more detailed and precise than could be gleaned hitherto from all the available literary and scattered documentary material together.

I do not suggest that these two groups of texts could have been fruitfully analysed without the other evidence. My point is that *only groups of documents* provide the essential elements of homogeneity and of duration of time.[36] For short periods, Kula has noted, 'we almost always have the impression of direction-less variations', especially in pre-capitalist societies where 'many economic indices are subject to great fluctuations in the short run and only to very slow change in the direction of the trend'.[37] However, when a series is available we have a check on the impression of directionless variations (or of stability); only then can the ancient historian take a step towards serial history. That it can never be more than a step is my reason for speaking of 'quasi- (or even pseudo-) statistical study'.

I deliberately selected as my examples two groups of docu-ments with minimum contents in order to underscore the qualita-tive change that the mere existence of groups brings to our study. Of course groups of documents that also have genuine contents can be more productive, but they are few in number and surprisingly neglected as groups.[38] Ampolo has properly pro-tested that the considerable scholarship devoted to the Athenian financial documents of the fifth century BC (which include the tribute lists) 'is mostly restricted to the field of *histoire événemen-tielle*, when it is not simply concerned with problems of the Athenian calendar'.[39] The neglect has become nothing short of a scandal in the case of the unparalleled documentation from the two great temple-centres, Delos and Delphi: one need only contrast the dismal scholarly record of the past half-century with the enormously promising previous half-century in both cases.

In closing, I should say explicitly that I am making no plea for turning a computer loose to register every number that comes its way. It is well known that many calculations which are in the technical sense 'statistically significant' are historically valueless. I ask only that the historian approach his material with significant questions in mind. Documents themselves ask no questions, though they sometimes provide answers.

[4]

'How it really was'[1]

After Edmund Wilson had embarked on his 'study of the writing and acting of history', from Vico to Trotsky, which was published under the title *To the Finland Station*, he received a letter in 1934 from his favourite teacher, Christian Gauss, the famous Princeton dean and professor of French, the burden of which was that out of Leopold von Ranke and the early Michelet 'came the school of scientific, dispassionate, objective history'. This, Gauss continued, 'I would call the archaeological interest' which 'indicates a lowering of vitality . . . the literature of escape', exemplified by the excitement over the discovery of the tomb of King Tutankhamen or Schliemann's hunt for Troy. 'Remember', he concluded, 'that Periclean Athens had no museum of antiques.'[2]

To write of Ranke with such pejorative overtones was rare in the 1930s, as it is still rare today, and a critique such as that by Gauss goes unnoticed and unanswered. Instead one can read in almost any history of history that Ranke was the greatest historian of the nineteenth century, the greatest master of 'scientific' history since Thucydides, *ad infinitum*. And it is the case that no other historian has ever written so many scholarly works over such a vast range in time and place, 'a larger number of mostly excellent books', in Acton's judgment, 'than any man that ever lived'.[3] Whether or not he was the greatest historian in modern times, he was certainly the most erudite. And that has helped create a confusion of values: erudition of itself subconsciously warrants the rightness not only of the details of the account but also of the general conception of a trend, a period, an institution. After all, did he himself not say, in probably the most famous of all pronouncements about the nature of history, that his aim was not to judge but only to tell 'how it really was' (*wie es eigentlich gewesen*)?[4]

The parallel with Thucydides comes easily to mind, and indeed it has been drawn repeatedly, among others by Ranke himself.[5] There are problems: Ranke spent his life discovering and studying written sources, Thucydides only oral reports (at a time when there were so few written sources); Thucydides did not believe that the past was really discoverable beyond the span covered by living oral testimony, whereas Ranke devoted much of his energy to the early modern period, going back to the fifteenth century; Ranke was extremely and pervasively devout, Thucydides was at best indifferent to the gods. However, we may let these essential differences pass for the moment (without sinking into the egregious error of calling them 'almost negligible'[6]). What the two men are supposed to have shared was a passionate concern for the facts, for getting them right, and a 'personal self-effacement'[7] in their presentation. There lies the key to 'objective, scientific history', we are told, and I find it a remarkable act of faith that so many intelligent and knowledgeable students of history have believed that for so long.

Thucydides never divulged his sources of information (apart from the few occasions when he indicated personal involvement), and I have already pointed out the untenability of the notion that he kept himself out of sight throughout his account. Ranke's procedure with respect to his sources was necessarily different. They were written and more often than not unpublished, and he felt it necessary to indicate them, especially as he regularly insisted that establishment of the 'facts' was the first and essential duty of the historian. However, if one looks, for instance, at his 3-volume history of the popes, probably his most successful single work,[8] Ranke's practice is puzzling, not only by modern standards but also in more universal terms. In the preface, for instance, we are informed that most of the details of the reigns of Gregory XIII and Sixtus V, a period occupying some hundred pages, come from the Viennese archives; at the end there is a long catalogue of 185 manuscripts (between 1453 and 1783) consulted by Ranke, with some quotations and notes indicating their importance or reliability (a normal practice of his, with variants). In the text itself, however, there is very little specific citation of these sources for individual points, so little that it is not easy today to understand why these particular references were chosen. Short of going back to the original manuscripts, with only the most general indications of which might be relevant, the reader is unable to check the accuracy of Ranke's reporting of his facts, or the quality of his selection of data.[9]

I do not for a moment suspect Ranke of the slightest departure from absolute probity. However, it is inconceivable that anyone could copy or take notes from thousands of handwritten sources without ever copying incorrectly, and it is no less inconceivable that any man possessed an unerring eye for the essential item of information. In broader terms, Ranke's omissions, the narrowness of focus, are directly evident from his work. Croce, for example, pointed out that 'what in fact happened to the Catholic Church under the Counter Reformation of the Jesuits, how completely different it was from the Mediaeval Church; what happened to it during the spiritual decadence . . . until it reacted to the French Revolution by a fresh recovery, withdrawing from the upper classes among whom the Jesuits had worked in times past, to lean on the peasants and on remaining absolute governments; . . . Ranke does not investigate all this: he seems to be engaged rather in the fine art of embalming a corpse.'[10]

That verdict, not unlike Gauss' with which I opened, ran through a minority of Ranke's contemporaries and successors, including Heinrich Heine, Droysen and Jacob Burckhardt.[11] The aged Friedrich Meinecke, who had devoted half a century to holding up Ranke as the apogee of historiography, decided in his last work that 'today (1948) we are beginning to ask whether, in the end, Burckhardt will not have greater importance than Ranke for us as well as for later historians.'[12] The charge which they all levied was his lack of political toughness despite his anti-liberalism – Droysen wrote of him that 'he is much, very much talent, but little man'[13] – though that accusation was made from different and even opposing points of view (as with Heine and Droysen).

Political judgment of Ranke was not something external to, or

imposed upon, his historical writing. To think that is to be taken
in by the claim of self-effacement, to which Ranke himself contri-
buted powerfully and repeatedly. 'I have wished', he wrote in his
English History, 'to extinguish myself, so to speak, and to allow
only the things to speak.' Or again, 'Everything hangs together:
critical study of authentic sources; impartial view; objective description – the aim is the presentation of the whole truth.'[14] It
would not be difficult to quote literally hundreds of passages
which can be brought into a relationship with that statement of
methods and aim only by extraordinary contortions.[15] It will be
sufficient, however, to quote a few lines from the *History of the
Popes*. I could indeed restrict myself to the opening chapter on
Christianity in the Roman Empire, all of which is Ranke speaking, not 'things', but that would serve only to substantiate
Acton's sharp judgment that Ranke 'has never shown a knowledge of antiquity', and 'is wholly incapable of understanding the
ancient heathens or the medieval Christians, antiquity while
paganism was yet powerful'.[16] That, however, is not my intention. I am here concerned solely to exemplify Ranke's self-
projection by quoting from the sections on the Roman Inquisition
and on the St. Bartholomew's Day massacre in France:

'The most profound thinker of all, Giordano Bruno, a true
philosopher, after many persecutions and long wanderings, was
at last seized by the Inquisition, sent to Rome, imprisoned and
condemned to the flames, "not only", as the legal record sets
forth, "as a heretic, but as a dangerous heresiarch, who had
written things affecting religion, and unseemly".'[17]

'The investigation of physics and natural history was at that
time almost inseparably connected with philosophical inquiry.
The whole system of ideas as previously accepted was called into
question; there was indeed among the Italians of that period an
earnest tendency towards the vigorous pursuit of truth, a zeal for
progress, a noble loftiness of anticipation. Who shall say to what
glorious results this might have led? But the Church set up a
barrier which they must not overpass; woe to him who should be
found beyond it.'[18]

Both quotations, which are complete, have been taken from a

section that has puzzlingly been called 'impressive' for its 'sophistication'.[19] There is not a word about Bruno's ideas or why he was a 'true philosopher', nothing about the 'earnest tendency' among contemporary Italians 'towards the vigorous pursuit of truth' and the like. Even the potted cultural chapters in present-day textbook histories do better than that.

The short paragraph closing the half a dozen pages on the anti-Huguenot campaign in sixteenth-century France, climaxed by the St Bartholomew's Day massacre, is an example of another kind, requiring no comment: 'But can it be possible that crimes of a character so sanguinary can ever succeed? Are they not in too flagrant opposition to the more profound mysteries of human events (*Dinge*), to the undefined yet inviolable and ever active principles that govern the order of nature? Men may blind themselves for a time, but they cannot disturb the moral laws on which their existence reposes; these rule with a necessity as inevitable as that which regulates the course of the stars.'[20]

Now, though the title of this chapter is taken from Ranke, he is not its subject. I must stress that I have made no discovery or said anything about Ranke that could not have been noticed and said by any reasonably attentive reader. Why, then (to repeat a question I have already posed), has there been such a persistent faith in the self-effacement of Ranke and other historians like him, beginning of course with Thucydides? I suggest that the answer is tied to the equally firm view that Thucydides and Ranke were paragons of 'objective' or 'scientific' history; that the objective historian is someone who effaces himself and lets 'things' speak directly to the reader. It is also worth noticing in this context, that there is surprisingly little immediate evidence for the famed accuracy of Ranke, almost none for Thucydides. They were so obviously men of extreme earnestness in their concern for the truth that we believe them when they insist on the strenuous efforts they have made to get things right.

I do not propose to challenge that faith, but I must make the simple point that accuracy and truth are not synonymous. Whether he was correct or not, Lord Acton was neither para-doxical nor nonsensical in the following judgment of Ranke: 'No historian has told fewer untruths, few have committed so few mistakes. None is a more unsafe guide. All that he says is often true, and yet the whole is untrue, but the element of untruth is difficult to detect . . . Ranke deceives not by additions but by selection.'[21] 'Facts' are not brute objects lying 'there' to be discovered (found) by the historian: not even Ranke believed that, much though he may have written as if he did. '*Wie es eigentlich gewesen*' meant the right portrayal of relations. Historians, wrote Droysen, 'must know what they wish to seek; only then will they find something. One must question things (*Dinge*) correctly, then they give an answer.'[22] The corollary is that one may question incorrectly; then the whole becomes untrue regardless of the accuracy of the individual facts within (or underlying) the whole.

Since Droysen, so far as I know, the only historian of antiquity to have discussed basic questions of methodology systematically and at length was Eduard Meyer (until, that is, Momigliano embarked on his long career of research and writing about historiography, which is a cognate but rather different subject). Meyer did it on three different occasions, twice in long general essays and once in a monograph on Thucydides, who was for him the model historian, followed by Ranke.[23] Meyer continued into the twentieth century the 'golden age' of nineteenth-century German historiography. He was immensely erudite and productive, convinced to the point of dogmatism that political history deservedly claimed absolute priority, extremely conservative in his political views, and, in the years during and following the First World War, fiercely chauvinistic.[24] Philosophically, however, he was not particularly competent (not too blunt a phrase) and his excursion into the philosophy of history was demolished by Max Weber, who said at one point in his critique, that 'all the admirers of his great work will rejoice that he cannot proceed at all seriously with these ideas, and they hope that he will not even attempt to do so for the sake of an erroneously formulated theory'.[25]

Weber's critique was thus at the same time a tribute to Meyer's standing and indeed greatness as an historian. And even those of us who are rather less enthusiastic cannot dispute Meyer's importance, or the importance of his writing on historical method

For he did nothing less than deny the existence of canons with which to judge a historian's work, even the work of the incomparable Thucydides, insisting that 'great' historians must be accepted on faith. Historiography is not a 'systematic discipline', the historical method is unteachable and is anyway overrated.[26] Free will and chance (*Zufall*) dominate causality; anyone who fails to appreciate that 'not only destroys everything that constitutes the main object of historical interest but also does away with its essence completely and replaces it by formulae . . . lacking any concrete content'.[27] The historian's choice of material is entirely a matter for his decision: criticism of the silences of, for instance, Thucydides cannot be tolerated; 'the historian's subjective judgment, only the conception he himself has of his art can be decisive. The historian has the right to demand that in this respect he is not judged differently from the artist.'[28] The key is the historian's intuition. In a lengthy analysis of Thucydides' speeches, with the familiar claim that they permit the reader to form his own judgments – that is the foundation of what 'is meant by the objectivity of Thucydides' – we are told that 'the task which he set himself, is to allow the things to affect us immediately, as they are, and that is nothing other than how they appear to him himself'.[29] Ranke has in a way been sharpened and indeed brutalized: objectivity is what the historian holds to be true. There is, says Meyer, no other kind of history.

Judging history against poetry goes back at least to Aristotle (in a famous passage in the *Poetics*, chapter 9) who pronounced the latter to be more weighty, more philosophical.[30] Behind that judgment lay the problem that has exercised historians (and others) ever since, of how to draw truths, general (or universal) truths, from the particulars which are held to be the only proper subject-matter of history. It was the romantic idealistic school of German historians of the nineteenth century, so far as I know, who found the answer by making a significant switch in the history-poetry relationship, from judging one against the other to equating the two partially: in his choice of material, said Meyer, the historian must be given the same rights as the artist. This was no mere figure of speech; Meyer was stating an epistemological principle, the role of the imagination as a means of discovering the truth 'as it really was'.

The central ideas of the new historical school were first adumbrated by Wilhelm von Humboldt, patron-saint of the new University of Berlin and of the Berlin Academy. He opened a lecture 'On the Historian's Task', given at the Academy in 1821 and published in the following year, with a formulation not too different from Ranke's *wie es eigentlich gewesen*. 'The historian's task', said Humboldt, 'is to present what actually happened (*die Darstellung des geschehenen*). The more purely and completely he achieves this, the more perfectly has he solved his problem. A simple presentation is at the same time the primary, indispensable condition of his work, the highest achievement he will be able to attain. Regarded in this way, he seems to be merely receptive and reproductive, not himself active and creative.' However, Humboldt continued, an event 'is only partially visible in the world of the senses; the rest has to be added by intuition, inference, and guesswork . . . The truth of any event is predicated on the addition . . . of that invisible part of every fact, and it is that part, therefore, which the historian has to add . . . Differently from the poet, but in a way similar to him, he must work the collected fragments into a whole.'[31]

It is no longer easy to appreciate the reasons for Humboldt's overwhelming impact on the intellectual and cultural life of nineteenth-century Germany. Although much of his writing, apart from his work on linguistics and language theory, was fragmentary or published posthumously, he laid the foundations of the modern German university, he fostered the 'new' classical humanism, and he provided the leading ideas, or at least the central approach, of the dominant trend in German historiography for a century or more. Yet Droysen, who proclaimed that it was Humboldt who had showed him the way to correct historical understanding and practice – he was the Francis Bacon of the historical disciplines – conceded that one 'may not speak of a philosophical system of Humboldt's' but only of a *Weltanschauung*, and he thought it necessary to develop methods that would control intuition and other kinds of subjectivism.[32] Ranke, who obviously knew the lecture on the historian's task (which he echoed in the introduction to his own first book, published two years later) and who could not have escaped Humboldt's ideas and perhaps his physical presence in the two famous Berlin salons that he frequented, those of Rahel Varnhagen von Ense and of Bettina von Arnim, surprisingly, and indeed rather mysteriously, failed to mention him in any writing.[33] That there was an intellectual filiation is nevertheless certain, close enough to justify Georg Iggers in heading two successive chapters (3 and 4) of his *The German Conception of History*, 'The Theoretical Foundations of German Historicism I: Wilhelm von Humboldt' and 'II. Leopold von Ranke'.[34]

There has been, perhaps most pronounced in the United States at the turn of the century, a persistent misconception of Ranke as the 'father of scientific history', the model historian who was 'determined to hold strictly to the facts of history, to preach no sermon'.[35] Did the pedants who reduced Ranke's historiography to such 'soulless positivism' ever read him, one wonders, or were they content with parroting *wie es eigentlich gewesen*? Behind that gross misunderstanding there of course lay the long familiar hankering of the academic humanist for the certainties of the natural sciences. One sympathizes with that, with the efforts to escape from Eduard Meyer's conversion of objectivity into subjectivity, with his parallel between the historian and the artist, with his stress on intuition. But complete honesty, respect for and critical evaluation of evidence, are only necessary conditions for history-writing as for science; they are not sufficient conditions for either. Accuracy, Housman once wrote about textual criticism, is a duty, not a virtue.[36]

Discussions of the issues have burgeoned in recent decades. Many are philosophically sophisticated, complex and at times difficult, but others seem to me to be barely or not at all qualified. For one thing there is a linguistic confusion: French *science*, German *Wissenschaft*, perhaps less so English *science*, need mean no more than a discipline or field of study pursued systematically and rigorously. In that sense the study of history may be included among the 'sciences', but I fail to see that such a classification gets us very far, or indeed anywhere. When Hajo Holborn, for example, says that 'to talk of a science of history means nothing but an affirmation of the critical and systematic approach to history, and the validity of the results achieved in this way',[37] he avoids the fundamental question: How does one assess the validity of the 'results' achieved? We know how to do that in physics or biology or astronomy – but how in history?

The consequences can become grotesque, as when we read in a book entitled *Thucydides and the Science of History* that the speeches 'represent the attempt of Thucydides to do for history what Hippocrates was at the same time trying to do for medicine . . . Through the symptoms to arrive at a general description and thence to penetrate, if possible, to the true classification of the malady, this is the procedure which Hippocrates advocates and which he designates by the words *semeiology* and *prognosis*. But this was the very process which Thucydides sought to apply to history, which thus for him becomes the semeiology and prognosis of human life.'[38]

Thucydides no doubt thought that unchanging human nature was likely to lead to recurrence of behaviour patterns when the circumstances repeated themselves, that he had pointed to some of the regularities, and that therefore he was offering a prognosis. Nevertheless, I fail to comprehend how any historian can seriously have compared the Hippocratic *Epidemics* with Thucydides' account of the plague, let alone with the speeches in Thucydides. It has been demonstrated that even the vocabulary of the historian's pages on the plague at Athens 'is not entirely, is not even largely, technical', despite the distinguished list of commentators who have claimed that it is.[39] In any event, a 'scientific' vocabulary is an irrelevance in this context. We no longer take the simplistic view that a science requires experimentation and predictability, but on any view every science studies regularities, phenomena that repeat themselves and can be observed repeatedly, by different observers under controlled conditions, through a 'continual refining away of irrelevant factors'. 'Things are otherwise with the historian', continues Patrick Gardiner in his now classic book on the nature of historical explanation. 'His aim is to talk about what happened on particular occasions in all its rarity, all its richness, and its terminology is adapted to this object. That is the reason why terms like "revolution" are left so vague and so open. They are accommodating terms, able to cover a vast number of events falling within an indefinitely circumscribed range.'[40] Hence even the word 'because' has a different meaning, or rather range of meanings, in historical explanation than in the sciences: it may legitimately refer to a motive, for example, an emotional state or an interest.[41]

I shall argue that the fairly traditional Gardiner view of history needs some qualification. Nevertheless, I accept that the concept of scientific history is applicable only in a restricted sense, so much so that it is doubtful that it fills much useful purpose other than to give the historian whatever aesthetic or moral satisfaction he may derive from the label 'scientific'. It is, furthermore, becoming increasingly apparent, at least to many of us, that the claims of sociology and anthropology to scientific status are also restricted, for, like history, each 'is a consumer of laws, not a producer of them'.[42] I say this with confidence despite the apparent testimony in the other direction in the enormous development of quantitative history (or serial history or cliometrics), for which the label 'scientific' is claimed by its practitioners.[43] A brief consideration will show why I take the stand I do.

What does cliometric history produce? At best, it provides correlations and other statistical data with a low margin of error; that is to say, it provides evidence of probabilities or trends, but it tells us nothing about individual cases (other than the probabilities) and it provides no explanations of past human behaviour and institutions, or at least no generalized explanations. Even if we agree for purposes of the present discussion that Fogel and Engerman have demonstrated that slave labour was efficient in the American South, that does not warrant any implication that slave labour was equally efficient in Italy in the last centuries of the Republic or the early Empire; nor can it tell us a great deal about the causes of the American Civil War or about the introduction of slavery in the first instance.

And that is cliometric history at its best, when it is coping with narrowly defined questions of fact and is employing generally agreed methods (and data) in the search for answers. 'The behaviour that cliometricians have dealt with so far', Fogel has recently pointed out, 'has generally been represented by single equations or by simple simultaneous equation models *with relatively few variables*'[44] (my italics). It is precisely by reducing the number of variables to be examined that cliometrics has best established its claim to being scientific and has produced its best work. But, it is not unfair to add, by so doing it has also paid the price of 'leaving out the greater part of what is known of the lives of human beings who are in this way recorded'.[45]

Some years ago, at a small conference on historical methods, I protested the claim of one of the doyens of serial history that we are now able for the first time to write a history of the family, thanks to modern demographic study. 'All the possible statistics', I wrote subsequently, 'about age of marriage, size of family, rate of illegitimacy will not add up to a history of the family'.[46] To which blunt (and bold) assertion, Robert Fogel has recently expressed his agreement: 'history must deal fully with a series of issues about the quality of family life . . . the changing roles of husbands, wives, and other kin and of relationships between them; their changing attitudes toward each other; and the effects of family attitudes and roles, first on the culture of families and the fate of its individual members, and ultimately on the society, economy, and the state . . . Can it be denied that a satisfactory history of the family must have both qualitative and quantitative aspects, and that neglect of either may lead the historian astray?'[47]

Fogel went on to conclude that the 'anticipated rout of traditional historians has not materialized and history has not been transformed into a science. Cliometricians have had to acknowledge that there are issues for which traditional methods are better suited than scientific ones . . . whether cliometrics opens up new avenues of knowledge, overturns particular elements in the traditional narrative, or merely refines some elements, the contribution is to the elaboration of the narrative. Cliometrics has not made narrative history obsolete. The genuine differences between "scientific" and traditional historians over subject matter, methods, and style should not obscure their numerous and more fundamental affinities and complementarities.'[48]

This statement, of the utmost importance, brings us back, by a different route, to the point I have already made in connection with history and archaeology, namely, that the study of the human past is a single subject with varied techniques depending on the kinds of questions being asked, the kinds of evidence that are available, and the methods of presentation that are appropriate. Undue stress in recent years on the difference between narrative and serial history, like the current demand for a revival of the narrative (which does not seem to be in any need of the kiss of life),[49] is fundamentally misleading. All forms of historical discourse, including the most austere narrative, constantly classify, conceptualize, generalize: behind the collection of data and their ordering in a sequence there lies a series of judgments flowing from the historian's understanding of 'relationships to longer enduring factors which are not themselves links in the sequential chain of events which constitute the "story".[50] The form of discourse chosen is not a free or arbitrary one: it depends on the questions being asked and on the material available at least as much as on the temperament or 'style' of the individual historian.

All this leads to the conclusion that both modes of research, in Fogel's terminology the 'scientific' and the 'traditional', must be consciously and conscientiously deployed. It is no longer permissible to offer an account of the American Civil War without a clear, detailed statement about the relative efficiency and profitability of slave labour, and that can be achieved only by cliometric procedures. On the other hand, to think that cliometrics will make possible a proper history of the Civil War is as fallacious as the notion that we can now write a 'scientific' history of the family. 'To explain the outbreak of the Civil War,' Fogel wrote, 'one must deal not only with systematic forces in the economic, social, ideological, and political spheres that may have made such a crisis likely, but also with the role of particular personalities, unique events, decisions that may well have gone differently, blunders, and a host of other contingent factors that loomed large in the actual course of events.'[51] Unfortunately this is a recommendation that the historian of antiquity cannot put into practice in a literal way. The necessary data are unavailable except in a small number of situations, even fewer if we seek a series over a longer period of time. The literary sources provide none, or virtually none; only documents and archaeological finds enter into consideration, and I have already given a few examples of the latter.[52] But the limits are quickly reached: it is unimaginable, for example, that we shall ever attain to a quantitative presentation of the productivity or efficiency of slave labour in ancient Greece or Rome.

However, this ineradicable weakness does not mean that the ancient historian has no escape from the romantic-idealistic tradition that stretches from Humboldt to Eduard Meyer and beyond, with its stress on chance, 'free will' and intuition; its linking the historian with the artist, not merely in the rhetorical dress with which they both present their material but also epistemologically, in their freedom to make decisions about the selection of material to be included or excluded, in their unchallengeable right to do so on the basis of their intuition, their conscience, or whatever; its arbitrary conversion of objectivity into its opposite, subjectivity. The ancient historian cannot be a cliometrician in a serious way, but he can resort to a second-best procedure through the use of non-mathematical models, thereby controlling the subject of his discourse by selecting the variables he wishes to study. A model has been defined as 'a simplified structuring of reality which presents supposedly significant relationships in a generalized form. Models are highly subjective approximations in that they do not include all associated observations or measurements, but as such they are valuable in obscuring incidental detail and in allowing fundamental aspects of reality to appear. This selectivity means that models have varying degrees of probability and a limited range of conditions over which they apply.'[53]

For the traditional historian, the models that are perhaps most familiar and that have had the longest career are one or two of Max Weber's ideal types. An ideal type is a model: that has to be said bluntly and sharply because of a persistent misconception that pervades contemporary historical literature. One quotation will be in order from Weber's fullest statement on ideal types because it expresses clearly the nature and function of models in an historical inquiry. 'An ideal type is achieved by the one-sided *accentuation* of one or more points of view and by the synthesis of many diffuse, discrete, more or less present and occasionally absent *individual* phenomena, which are arranged according to those one-sidedly emphasized viewpoints into a unified mental construct. In its conceptual purity, this mental construct can never be found empirically in reality. It is a *utopia*. *Historical* research faces the task of determining in each *individual* case, the extent to which this ideal-construct approximates to or diverges from reality, to what extent, for example, the economic structure of a certain city is to be classified as a "city-economy".'[54]

Except among economic historians, however, model-construction is a rare procedure among historians, especially so, I suspect, among ancient historians (though a growing number of classical archaeologists have begun to turn to models under the stimulus of the 'new archaeology'). Indeed, the signs are unmistakable that the reverse is taking place precisely in the field that Weber mentioned, the history of cities. Instead of efforts to establish clearer patterns of city behaviour through the employment of simplifying assumptions, there has emerged in recent decades a spate of pseudo-histories of ancient cities and regions in which every statement or calculation to be found in an ancient text, every artefact finds a place, creating a morass of unintelligible, meaningless, unrelated 'facts' (which I write in inverted commas because many of the so-called facts are pure guesses or outright fictions). Two recent developments lie behind this trend, firstly, the burgeoning publication of inscriptions, papyri, archaeological reports, and, secondly, the introduction of the computer, especially into prosopography. The old problem of establishing canons of selection and of settling who determines them has been 'solved' by abolishing selection altogether. Everything now goes in, as if in answer to the familiar question in children's examinations, 'Tell all you know about X.'

This is such a serious charge, and the various methodological issues are in my view so important, that I must justify my claims at some length. I start with Fraser's *Ptolemaic Alexandria*, published in 1972, the best of the current crop of pseudo-histories of ancient cities, the model for the genre by the man who is also, in this country, the chief patron of such studies. *Ptolemaic Alexandria* is a paragon of erudite scholarship: that must be stressed at the outset. Its vital statistics are as follows: a text of more than 800 pages, an 1100-page volume containing 6036 notes plus 'some addenda', and a third volume with 157 pages of indexes. The text is in two parts, one, 'the framework' in five chapters, and two, 'the achievement', consisting of long essays on aspects of Alexandrian culture, including areas of admitted non-achievement (philosophy, historiography and drama).

Part I, 300 pages in length, alone concerns me, and I can best characterize it simply by a few short quotations from each of its five chapters:

Chapter 1, 'Foundation and Topography', concludes by saying that 'our study . . . reveals one limitation, . . . the development of Alexandria as a city largely escapes us' (p.36).

Chapter 2, 'The Population, Its Organization and Composition', requires two quotations: 'over the origins of the population of Alexandria a darkness reigns, through which, at present, scarcely one chink of light gleams' (p.62), an ignorance that is 'only slightly mitigated by our knowledge regarding the measures taken to increase that body in the Ptolemaic period' (p.65). The extent of that mitigation could hardly have been less, for it consists of a single, not very comprehensible item, the admission in the third century BC and the first half of the second of Greeks and Macedonians in the Fayum into the Alexandrian citizen-body as demesmen, under unknown conditions and with unknown effects.

Chapter 3, 'City and Sovereign', opens by confessing that 'our ignorance of the organization of the Alexandrian citizen-body is matched by our ignorance about the constitution by which the body was governed' (p.93).

4, 'Of trade and industry in Alexandria we know very little', not even whether Alexandrian trade was royal trade or private trade or both (p.135).

And finally, the relatively more 'abundant' evidence for Alexandrian cults has 'virtually no trace' of the large native population of the city (p.189). Fraser finds it 'probable that this silence corresponds to a lack of religious activity on the part of the Egyptian population'. I find that as improbable a guess as one can imagine.

It hardly needs saying explicitly that on such a foundation of solid ignorance it was possible to produce a 300-page text only by the tell-all-you-know technique. Nor is it necessary to explain at any length that such anachronistic antiquarianism is uncontaminated by any contact with the large and often insightful literature on the sociology and history of cities in general. I have learned to take that for granted, but the bland lack of curiosity still puzzles me. I give one quite crucial illustration.

The sole population figure that we have for Alexandria is that of Diodorus, who says (17.52.6) that when he visited the place (in 60 BC) he was informed by the officials in charge of the census that the free population was over 300,000. Beloch accepted this figure, arbitrarily added 200,000 slaves and came to a total of half a million.[55] Fraser says that the figure cannot be accorded 'statistical value', but he accepts Diodorus' further statement that Alexandria was the most populous city in the world (though elsewhere the same author says that most people ranked it first or second; 1.50.7), plucks out of the air Kahrstedt's guess of 900,000 for Rome, and concludes therefore that the total population of Alexandria was 'hardly, if at all, short of a million', a figure it would have reached some time in the second century BC.[56] The wonder of this picture seems not to have occurred to Fraser (or others writing on the subject). Such a rate of growth is without a single parallel in the history of the west; even London required 200 years, from 1600 to 1800, to jump from about 200,000 inhabitants to 900,000,[57] and London was unique, at least in the western world. For such a leap to have occurred, it has been estimated that London required a net immigration of 8000 people a year and at times substantially more over the entire period. Furthermore, the food requirements of such a rapidly swelling population had catalytic effects on agriculture in Kent, East Anglia and Hertfordshire, and even beyond.

I have spoken of a puzzling, bland lack of curiosity. Even the half-a-million figure ought to have aroused some interest, some questions; the arbitrary doubling of the figure merely compounds the difficulties several times over. Where did such a vast inflow of permanent migrants come from, and how were they recruited and settled? How was the food supply of this great urban complex organized? Where were the sources of supply? These questions are not even posed seriously. We may not be able to provide satisfactory answers, but the implications, or at least the possibilities, can and ought to be suggested. To write (p.135) that 'in any case the regional differentiae of large towns within one cultural area are slight. In the period before mechanized transport many of the everyday demands of such cities were naturally met by local produce, and this feature must simply be taken for granted in Alexandria as elsewhere' is at best a complete evasion. Alexandria was not just another 'large town': it was one of the two or three super-cities of the ancient Mediterranean world. Nor was its hinterland capable of feeding anything like half a million people.

In fact, we effectively never hear of the hinterland or of local agricultural production at any point in the book. Fraser is too obsessed with the widely shared notion that from the outset Alexander had before him the vision of the future commercial capital of the Mediterranean (even before he had defeated and conquered the Persian Empire). He begins his account with the frequently repeated fable that Alexander marked out the perimeter of his future city with meal which the soldiers were carrying, because he and his builders lacked suitable material. The Greek text of Arrian (3.2.1–2) is even given in full, ending with the prophecy of a soothsayer that the city would be prosperous. On that Fraser comments that Arrian's account 'indicates the motive of Alexander – commercial prosperity', for which there is not a word in the text, but he mysteriously omits the nine final words, 'that the city would be prosperous in general, but particularly in the fruits of the earth'. The possibility is never raised that the ancient authorities, writing 300–600 years after the event, were reading back to the foundation the later history of the city, or that the normal first step in any new ancient foundation was settlement of the newcomers on the land.[58]

In the past two or three decades there has been a great new outburst of urban history, quite sophisticated in its theoretical underpinning and its employment of statistical methods. It would be nice to think that Fraser and his pupils and followers were responding in the ancient field to the new urban history, but I fear that this is not the case. In the 1930s and 1940s the Johns Hopkins University in the United States had already published a comparable series of monographs, under the sponsorship of David Robinson. The excuse then was the availability of a mass of archaeological evidence; the excuse now is rather the availability of a quantity of epigraphical evidence. One suspects, alas, that the compelling motive is no more than the desire to find new subjects, especially for Ph.D. candidates. Certainly I am unaware of any discussion in this literature of principles, concepts, ideas of urbanism in classical antiquity or of any concern for what is happening in the medieval and modern fields in this respect.

I must say again, emphatically, that I have selected for more detailed comment the most learned, most massive book of its genre. Nothing would be gained by examining in the same way the whole crop of the more recent city-histories or regional histories – whether of Argos, Boeotia, classical and Hellenistic Byzantium, Capua, Corinth, Cos, Marseilles, Potidaea, Olbia or Thebes – but it may be worth a moment to look at Roman regional accounts. 'Like any other area', we read, 'Samnium underwent a continuous and persistent development . . . We cannot document the changes in detail' (which means simply that we cannot document them), 'but it is clear that contact with the Romans had some influence on political concepts, the proximity of Campania on commercial life and cultural growth, and the example of the Greeks on religious beliefs'.[59] Of which Italic people in the southern half of Italy can that not be said? And what does it actually say? Or of which future province of the Roman Empire can it not be said, with the requisite variations, that the economic life (of Noricum in this instance) 'depended on agricultural production, pastoralism, mining, industry – above all iron-smelting and metal-working – and trade'?[60] Only the style varies, not the substance: in place of Fraser's open and repeated confessions of ignorance, we are more commonly offered a code that serves as a synonym, the repeated employment of 'doubtless', 'no doubt', 'must have been'.

None of this latter-day antiquarianism, it should be stressed, is a traditional narrative. Although there are bits of narrative stretches embedded in it, mostly dealing with individual battles or revolts that receive a mention, by Herodotus or Diodorus or Livy for instance, the great bulk is in fact concerned with institutions. As such, it falls between all possible stools. It is obviously not cliometric or serial in any possible sense; it asks no questions other than antiquarian ones; it merely tells all the author knows. And, by avoiding analytical constructs, it falls headlong into the trap long ago predicted by Max Weber: 'the inevitable consequence is either that he (the historian) consciously or unconsciously uses other similar concepts *without* formulating them verbally and elaborating them logically or that he remains stuck in the realm of the vaguely "felt"'.[61] Illustrations are available in numbers beyond counting, though perhaps not so often accompanied by proud boasts of a refusal to be tempted by 'preconceived notions derived from other . . . systems'.[62]

It is in the nature of models that they are subject to constant adjustment, correction, modification or outright replacement. Non-mathematical models have few if any limits to their usefulness: whereas cliometric models are restricted to quantitative data, there is virtually nothing that cannot be conceptualized and analysed by non-mathematical models – religion and ideology, economic institutions and ideas, the state and politics, simple descriptions and developmental sequences. The familiar fear of *a priorism* is misplaced: any hypothesis can be modified, adjusted or discarded when necessary. Without one, however, there can be no explanation; there can be only reportage and crude taxonomy, antiquarianism in its narrowest sense.

[5]

War and Empire[1]

In the opening of Plato's *Laws*, the Cretan speaker, Clinias, says that 'what most men call peace is merely an appearance; in reality all cities are by nature in a permanent state of undeclared war against all other cities' (626A). It would be difficult to collect a numerous list of dissenters to this statement, in effect none from the ancient world[2] and surprisingly few in modern times despite the considerable outpouring ever since the sixteenth century of works deploring war or seeking to curb its excesses. Within the past century anthropologists seem to have largely agreed among themselves that the statement does not hold for very simple societies; that war is a product of civilization. Perhaps, but the fact remains that all historical peoples have in that sense been 'civilized' societies who fought wars with unrelenting frequency.

In the case of the Greeks and Romans, the correct phrase is indeed 'unrelenting regularity'. According to Livy (1.19.2–3), the temple of Janus had been closed (signifying that 'there was peace with all neighbouring peoples') only twice in the whole history of the Republic; once in the mid-third century BC at the end of the first Punic War, and again after Augustus' defeat of Antony and Cleopatra in 30 BC. The Greeks had no such symbol, but it can be shown that Athens alone was at war on average more than two years out of every three between the Persian wars and the defeat by Philip of Macedon at Chaeronea in 338 BC, and that it never enjoyed ten consecutive years of peace in all that period. The picture was even grimmer during the three Hellenistic centuries, following the eastern conquests of Alexander, though no calculation is possible. The forty-odd years that were required to bring some sort of stability into the Hellenistic east exhausted the manpower and resources of both Macedonia and old Greece. Yet 'fratricidal struggles' never ceased thereafter, 'in a sterile task . . . by which the Hellenistic world committed suicide'.[3]

The Roman statistics are especially staggering. On one calculation, in the half-century of the Hannibalic and Macedonian wars,
ten per cent and often more of all adult Italian males were at war
year by year, a ratio that rose during the wars of the first century
BC to one in every three males. On another calculation, more than
half of all Roman citizens regularly served in the army for seven
years in the early second century BC. These figures are approximations, or even partly guesses, to be sure, but they are of the
right order.[4] The accompanying ideology was complex, but the
dominant component was that war stimulated the highest virtues, a doctrine that is familiar enough in the modern world. For
the latter, it is enough to quote Jacob Burckhardt: 'A people
finally learns its full national strength only in war, in a comparative struggle against other peoples . . . A long peace leads to
enervation.'[5] Such notions coexisted in antiquity (again as today)
with expressions of the tragic side of warfare, with images of a
golden age without war, with a condemnation of 'civil war',
extended to the vain plea that Greeks ought not to fight other
Greeks and later to the prevention of war within the Roman
empire. But the *pax Romana* never included the peoples outside
the confines of Roman rule.

That none of these 'peaceful' sides of the ideology weakened
what I have called the dominant component is perhaps most
neatly revealed in ancient religion. Neither the enormously
powerful Roman Mars nor the weaker Greek Ares received the
slightest competition from the minor divinities of peace. It was
always assumed that divine support was available for a war, and
the mythology is replete with the satisfaction shown by the gods
in the prowess and the military successes of their human pro-
tégés. Nor is it on record, to the best of my knowledge, that the
gods through their oracles and signs ever recommended peace
for its own sake (though they sometimes advised against a
specific battle or war for given reasons).

Regardless of ideological nuances, it was universally accepted
in antiquity that war is a natural condition of human society.
Neither historians nor philosophers ever asked the question,
Why war?, although after Herodotus and Thucydides had led the

way they regularly examined the reasons and pretexts for the outbreak of a particular armed conflict.[6] In those discussions some doubts appear, and some of the rules of the game indicate a certain conflict of values. When Polybius reflected contemporary concern about the rightness of the Roman decision, in response to the appeal of the Mamertine mercenaries settled in Messina (1.10–11), to embark on what became the first Punic War, or when he denounced the Roman seizure of Sardinia as being 'against all justice' (3.38.1), he raised no general moral problem nor did he challenge the truth of the proposition that war is a natural form of human behaviour. However, the Roman claim to fight only just wars, enforced through the fetial law, hypocritical though it became in practice, or the universal rule that burial of the enemy dead must be permitted, through a truce if necessary, reflected a genuine conflict of values; not a challenge to the idea that war is natural or to the place of military virtue in the scale of virtues in general, but an important nuance that complicates all problems relating to war and peace, even the historical problems of causes, of war-guilt.

The most important complication was the impossibility of wholly separating the question of why war takes place from the different question of the justness or injustice of any particular war. Sufficient illustration will be found in Thucydides, the ancient historian who, by unanimous agreement, took more care than any other in these matters. I refer to his account (1.66–88) of the debate in Sparta leading to the decision to declare war against Athens; to the controversial statement which appears to undermine his own detailed narrative of the prehistory of the war – 'the truest cause, in my view, the one least spoken of, was the fear induced in Sparta by the growing power of Athens, which made it necessary for the former to go to war' (1.23.6, cf. 1.88); or to his account of the debates leading to the Athenian invasion of Sicily in 415 BC, and in particular to his judgment of the motivation of Alcibiades, the chief promoter of the expedition, and of the citizens who voted for it in the Assembly (6.8–24). From these, and indeed from the whole of Thucydides' History, it emerges that war was always an option open in principle to any state; that, to formulate the same point in its obverse, any argument against going to war had to be based on concrete circumstances, not on a general objection, on a question of tactics, not of principle; that it was never easy to determine, either in advance or after the fact, exactly why a particular war came into being and that the rights or wrongs of a decision to go to war were neither easy to pin down nor necessarily commanding of wide support.

Despite the massive concern with war in ancient historical writing, it is significant that the analysis of causation failed to progress much. The 'fruit', Momigliano wrote, that Thucydides and his followers reaped 'is not very impressive. Neither Xenophon nor the author of the *Hellenica Oxyrhynchia* are at their best on the subject'; 'Polybius simplifies and rationalizes the causes of war'; Roman historians were not much better, nor were Plato and Aristotle in their theoretical reflections.[7] This failure he attributes to the underlying assumption that war is inevitable, a consequence of the nature of man, unlike the history of constitutions and constitutional struggles, which are man-made and therefore subject to change through human action.

Before we rush to deplore or condemn this failure, we must appreciate how little advance there has been since antiquity. The editor of an anthology on human conflict complained in 1945 that, 'despite the massive scrutiny that it has endured since the beginning of time, it remains as enigmatic as if its presence had not yet been detected by man'.[8] That is not hyperbolic (at least about classical antiquity), as it may seem at first glance. The central question is how one judges the use of violence as a 'normal' means of achieving a desired goal, individual or social. We live in a world which finds that ideologically and even morally objectionable, little though we may do about it in practice; that is fair enough until one blunderingly attributes similar values to the Greeks and Romans, among whom they were demonstrably absent. That was a world in which a large part of the labour force worked under various forms of non-economic compulsion, in which for a long period and over wide stretches of territory gladiatorial combats to the death provided the most popular form of public entertainment for the élites and the masses alike, in which brigandage and piracy and reprisals were often encouraged and even practised by 'civilized' governments.[9] It would therefore have been extraordinary if the prevailing ideology had failed to accept the 'naturalness' of warfare both as one means of acquisition and as one way of achieving other objectives. There is no need, on the evidence, to believe anything so odd about the Greeks and Romans. Yet there is and has been a powerful reluctance among historians to discuss ancient warfare and its consequences with a steady eye, undistorted by anachronistic ideological or psychological considerations, and it is worth a few moments to observe how far that situation still prevails.

I shall illustrate by a few examples chosen because they appeared to be obvious places in which to look for something better. First and perhaps most obvious is the opening volume, on Graeco-Roman antiquity, of Hans Delbrück's multi-volume *Geschichte der Kriegskunst*. Delbrück, successor to Treitschke as professor of history in Berlin, was a specialist on military history. Yet, despite the subtitle, 'within the framework of political history', the 500-page tome on antiquity says nothing on any serious historical problem; it is obsessed with the inaccuracy of the numbers in the ancient sources and is otherwise concerned above all with battle tactics and with army discipline.[10] Next we turn to Victor Martin's *La vie internationale dans la Grèce des cités* (1940), written in Geneva in the climate, if not directly under the auspices, of the international peace movement. Unlike Delbrück, Martin repeatedly offers explanations, brief, almost epigrammatic ones which in fact explain nothing, as a few quotations show: the defeat of Carthage at the battle of Himera produced only an ephemeral union in Sicily because of 'the jealousy of the tyrants towards the other dynasts' (p.14); Greece remained fragmented into city-states because that system 'corresponded so well to the secret tendencies of the Greek soul' (p.30); 'the ideal which animated all the Greek city-states is summed up in the word "liberty". All wished frenetically to enjoy this good in its fulness, and that sentiment determined the majority of their external political actions' (p.76).

And finally there is de Ste. Croix's recent massive *The Class Struggle in the Ancient Greek World* (published in 1981), which, despite the title, is devoted in more than a half to the Roman world, going down to the Arab conquest in the seventh century. The word 'war' does not appear in the index, and it would help little if it did because the references would be restricted to a few pages. He himself apologizes that he has had 'no space to discuss properly' what he calls 'the military factor', and when he gets round to devoting seven pages to it (259–66), they are obvious, fairly empty pages chiefly concerned with late antiquity. Elsewhere he quotes parenthetically Marx's remark that it was 'wars through which the Roman Patricians ruined the Plebeians' (p.335), but makes nothing of it. This is all peculiar (and to me inexplicable) for three reasons. First, in a book that is very polemically and aggressively Marxist, there is no development of Marx's ideas on war in the ancient world, which were not numerous but were far from negligible.[11] Secondly, it is hardly necessary to be a Marxist to appreciate the paramount role of war and empire (also largely ignored in the book) in the ancient 'class struggle'. Thirdly, de Ste. Croix's other book, written a decade previously (and published in 1972), was called *The Origins of the Peloponnesian War*. The sections directly devoted to origins hammer away at one thesis, namely, that it was the Spartans, not the Athenians, who were to blame for the outbreak of the long war which they eventually won. At one point (p.221), in the context of Athenian interest in the West that went back before the middle of the fifth century BC, he makes a throwaway concession which deserves extensive quotation.

'Of course any state will jump at every opportunity of extending its influence, and the Athenians could not be expected to reject requests for alliance which would, so to speak, enable them to "get a foot in the door", in case they should ever need a "legitimate" excuse for intervening in the West at some future date . . . Any large-scale Athenian move into Sicily would have a nakedly imperialistic character and was bound to arouse a great deal of opposition . . . It is understandable, therefore, that the Athenians should not even have begun to think seriously about gaining control of Sicily until after the Peloponnesian war had begun.'

It is unclear to me how a state can 'jump at every opportunity of extending its influence' without engaging in a move of a 'nakedly imperialistic character', one that would surely 'arouse a great deal of opposition'. In response to an appeal from its ally Leontini in 427 BC, the Athenians sent a substantial force to Sicily but could manage nothing more than desultory fighting for the next two years, whereas they responded to a similar Segestan request in 415 BC by mounting an invasion great enough to envisage taking over at least the eastern half of the island. Was the latter a more 'nakedly imperialistic' step than the former, or only a more powerful one? That it was far more powerful is beyond question: Thucydides (6.31.1) called the armada that sailed from Athens in 415 BC the most costly and splendid expedition that had ever been launched by a Greek state. But Thucydides was also un- ambiguous in his judgment of the earlier effort of 427: the Leontine alliance was a pretext, he explained (3.86.4), as the real Athenian aim was both to block Sicilian corn from reaching the Spartans and to test the possibility of bringing Sicily under Athenian subjection. 'Naked imperialism' is taken for granted. So is opposition; the practical question is whether or not that opposition can be overcome. Perhaps the second invasion was so powerful that it frightened off some potential Athenian allies within Sicily. But we shall never know, and anyway a distinction between a 'naked' and a 'more naked' imperialism does not seem very helpful.

De Ste. Croix has incorrectly injected his own value judgments into his account of ancient Greek behaviour. Moral approval or disapproval of a bellicose step (as with Polybius' disapproval of the Roman seizure of Sardinia), legitimate though it may be as an observer's judgment, cannot justifiably be introduced as a matter of course into the calculations of the actors. Marx himself avoided that mistake, as in the following statement:

'The only barrier which the community can encounter in its relations to the natural conditions of production as its own – to the land – is some *other community*, which has already laid claim to them as its inorganic body. War is therefore one of the earliest tasks of every primitive community of this kind, both for the defence of property and for its acquisition . . . Where man himself is captured as an organic accessory of the land and together with it, he is captured as one of the conditions of production, and this is the origin of slavery and serfdom, which soon debase and modify the original forms of all communities, and themselves become their foundation.'[12]

In effect, Marx extended and refined the commonplace that war is a 'natural' form of human behaviour by introducing the notion that, in early societies, war was the basic factor in economic growth and consequently in the transformation of the social structure. 'Military power', wrote Perry Anderson recently, 'was more closely tied to economic growth than in perhaps any other mode of production, before or since.' The 'full potential of the slave mode of production was the first time unfolded by Rome' in the early Empire, the 'predatory militarism' of the Republic having been 'its main lever of economic accumulation'.[13] That can also be agreed by historians who are not Marxists and who do not employ such concepts as 'mode of production'. For Roman history, at any rate, the evidence seems to me to be overwhelming.[14] Yet we are still being offered a regular diet of publications on the origins or causes of one or another Roman conflict, devoid of any general ideas about the nature of war and its motivations; in the case of Greek history, such publications occupy a position approaching monopoly. There are exceptions, of course, but the prevailing pattern cannot be determined by 'counting votes', X number of authors on one side, Y number on the other side.

I cannot claim to have looked at all possible publications, but it is the case that I know only two book-length works that systematically examine ancient warfare as a 'normal' structural component of ancient society, both written from a Marxist viewpoint. The first, published in 1901, was Ettore Ciccotti's *War and Peace in the Ancient World*, built on the thesis, stated several times, that, 'with the inadequate development of the productive forces, there was a tendency to shift to a system of violent appropriation

particularly against the outside world'.[15] Ciccotti was then a
major figure in Italian historical circles at a time when Marxism
was being vigorously debated, and Gaetano De Sanctis devoted
his Inaugural Lecture at Turin in 1904–5 to an attack on Marxism through a critique of Ciccotti's work, upholding a multi-causal
positivism against a Marxist dialectical approach. Ciccotti replied
in a pamphlet, 'The philosophy of war and the war against
philosophy', which enraged De Sanctis, who came back with a
long and admittedly bitter appendix to his original lecture, entitled 'Intorno al materialismo storico'. Croce then picked up the
debate briefly and with less sympathy for De Sanctis than one
might have anticipated, in the chapters on historical materialism
in his history of nineteenth-century Italian historiography, written in 1914 and 1915 but not published until 1921, and both the
discussion and Ciccotti's book itself then died, as far as I know.[16]
Half a century later, there appeared Yvon Garlan's *War in the
Ancient World*, and that book too seems to have struck little
resonance.

If war was indeed a central occupation of the ancient state, if
war was always one of the possible options, then the search for
the origins of an individual war is foredoomed so long as it
remains stuck in a narration of preceding events. Thucydides
demolished that approach in his brief phrase about the 'truest
cause' of the Peloponnesian War. Given Athenian expansion and
Spartan fear of it, war between the two was inevitable, and it was
a minor matter whether it broke out in one year rather than
another, over one incident rather than another. The inability of
historians today to achieve agreement about innumerable questions of that kind underscores the point.

But suppose we adopt the following approach? It can be agreed
without discussion that many wars were fought for mixed motives, for strictly defensive objectives, for psychological satisfac-
tions, such as glory or revenge, and for narrow tactical gains.
Wars were also fought out of fear, as Thucydides believed in the
case of the Peloponnesian War, and that is a particularly interesting motive because it demonstrates the truth of the proposition
that war was endemic, indeed 'natural', in this world. What was

there to fear? The possibility that another state would by use of force seek to raid and loot one's territory or to conquer, to subjugate in one way or another. These were far from imaginary, neurotic fears at any time in antiquity. For small states that is almost self-evident, but it is no less true, though paradoxical, for the most powerful imperialist or hegemonial states. One need only remember how easily the Romans, though exhausted by the Hannibalic War, were in 201 BC led by Rhodes and Pergamum into the so-called Third Macedonian War: one consideration in an indissoluble combination of motives was explicitly fear of a joint threat from Philip V of Macedon and Antiochus III in Syria.

But after we have listed all these varied motives, the hard fact remains that successful ancient wars produced profits, and that ancient political leaders were fully aware of that possibility. We may then ask, Who benefited? How were the profits distributed? With what effects? I do not suggest that the profit-motive mono-polized ancient thinking or policy-making with respect to war-fare, or even that it was always dominant in the motivation. There were many wars, especially petty ones, in which it was dominant, in which the old 'cattle-raid' quality stressed by the Homeric Nestor (*Iliad* 11.670–84) more or less summed up the whole story. These were the wars that received no extended attention in the sources (or the modern literature), and often none at all. At the other extremes, there were wars for the highest stakes, even the survival of one of the combatants, in which individual soldiers may have hoped for booty but in which such considerations could not have been the main, or even a main, component at the policy-making level (except *post factum*).

In between there was every kind of combination of motives. Even the Scythian expedition of Philip of Macedon in 339 BC, which we are explicitly told was designed to replenish the Macedonian coffers, an aim that Philip accomplished very satis-factorily, had political overtones as well.[17] Or the Roman 'punish-ment' of the seventy Epirot 'cities' who sided with King Perseus of Macedon in 167, took the form of almost unprecedented pillage, including the enslavement of 150,000 men, women and children. The state, writes Harris, which imposed an indemnity of 15,000 talents on Antiochus III and in a single day enslaved 150,000 Epirots is not to be called 'inert in enriching itself'.[18]

In his account of the preliminaries leading to the Peloponnesian War, Thucydides has an Athenian embassy in Sparta make the following argument about the establishment of the Athenian empire *and its retention* (1.76.2): 'We have done nothing extraordinary, nothing contrary to human practice, in accepting an empire when it was offered to us and then in refusing to give it up. Three very powerful motives prevent us from doing so – honour, fear and profit. And we were not the first to act in this way. It has always been the rule that the weak should be subject to the strong . . .' It was of course the expansion of the empire that was at the centre of the conflict over power which ultimately emerged as the Peloponnesian War.

In their accounts of ancient wars, modern historians fully acknowledge honour and fear, but too often not the profit-motive.[19] A curious ambivalence appears to have taken charge. In 1971 Pritchett introduced his chapters on booty in Greece with the sentence, 'No full-scale study of booty has ever been published.'[20] Yet Thucydides (6.24.3) explicitly listed the hope of profits as one motive behind the Athenian decision to invade Sicily in 415 BC; Aristotle (*Politics* 1256b23–26) no less explicitly included war among the 'natural' methods of acquisition; more and more epigraphical texts refer to treaties setting out in advance how the anticipated spoils should be divided among allies.[21] All this seems to drop from sight, or to be denigrated: 'If Rome entered the game for exploitation she did not play it well. Too many opportunities were missed . . .'[22] On the one hand, booty occasionally and mistakenly returns to the story on the most improbable and unattested occasions, such as the creation of the Delian League, which quickly became the Athenian empire.[23] However, apart from these strange and not too numerous anomalies, the standard histories of Greece and Rome normally pay little attention, and often none at all, to the material gains arising from warfare. Instead one finds a continuous succession of diplomatic and political events ending, for no sufficient reason, in a resort to arms.

Suppose, instead, we imagine that it is possible to construct a number of models of ancient wars? At the outset, we should have to distinguish between small and large states. A study of more than 2500 'important' modern European battles between 1480 and 1940 concluded that the frequency of participation by individual states ranged from 47% (France) to 2% (Denmark); that, 'clearly the great powers have been the most frequent fighters', while small states usually preferred to accept whatever was in store for them 'rather than to enter a war which would probably make their situation worse and to whose result they could contribute little.'[24]

It is a reasonable hypothesis that this was equally true, *mutatis mutandis*, of the ancient city-states, and a fairly recent study by Amit of three continuing struggles by small states to preserve their independence – Aegina against Athens, Plataea against Thebes, Mantinea against Sparta – offers detailed documentation. 'The Greek *polis*', writes Amit, 'was, in theory, a small independent unit aiming neither at expansion nor at conquest; every city, whatever its size or strength, was an equal and autonomous member of the Greek community. But in actual fact the great dominated the small . . . The struggle between the great powers of Greece for hegemony is only one aspect of Greek history, the perpetual conflicts between the small and the great cities are an equally important characteristic.'[25]

All this could be quantified further. The hypothesis I have just suggested could be checked by plotting systematically in these simple terms, of small and larger city-states, all the known wars or battles in archaic, classical and Hellenistic Greece until the Romans destroyed Greek independence. Such a chart would never achieve the statistical validity of Quincy Wright's analysis of modern European wars – the evidence is simply not there – but it should advance our understanding further than any study has achieved hitherto. It should either verify or falsify such a generalization as de Ste. Croix's in his book on the origins of the Peloponnesian War, in which he claims to be able to demonstrate, though he does not try to do so, that 'quarrels about the ownership of land, especially border land between two states, were the principal cause of war between Greek states'. Other 'types', he adds, 'are occasionally mentioned. For instance, Demosthenes (XV 170) speaks of wars "about hegemony": the Peloponnesian War was of that kind.'[26] But so were all the important ancient wars, at least from the introduction of mass armies in the later archaic age. There was no neat dichotomy into two 'types', one about the ownership of land, the other about hegemony. Such a conception is, in the end, a survival of the once prevailing and still tenacious nonsense that Rome, like Britain, acquired an empire in a fit of absence of mind.[27] Calling an empire a 'hegemony' does not change its nature or objectives in the slightest. Of course differences in the political power structures *within* hegemonial states constituted important variables. A Pericles, who was reelected *strategos* year after year, was differently motivated from an ambitious Roman consul who had only one year in which to acquire military glory and profit.

The model also requires the injection of costs and profits, two variables further qualified by the way they fell on, or accrued to, different sectors of the population. The importance of that qualification is quickly illustrated. In all the discussion in recent decades about the 'popularity of the Athenian empire',[28] there is a vital missing link; we do not know how the tribute paid to Athens was collected in the subject-states of the empire. If, as it is not unreasonable to assume, the customary practice of the classical Greek city-states prevailed, then the cost of the tribute fell entirely on the wealthier sector of the citizen-body, leaving the poor with no ground for resistance, or even objection, to Athenian hegemony on that score, which could be set against other factors that might favour their acceptance of the empire.

But the 'if' remains completely open in so far as any genuine evidence is concerned, and that particular lack of information bedevils most efforts to strike a balance-sheet of ancient warfare, conquest or empire. We know, for instance, that between, say, 367 and 30 BC, Rome collectively and many Romans individually enriched themselves vastly through the continuing warfare; we have some idea, though not too much, of the size of individual Roman fortunes in the early Empire; we know how much legionaries were paid and we can even make a reasonable guess at what it cost to feed and transport them for a campaigning season. But we cannot say what a campaign or a war cost, even in the most rudimentary monetary terms (without the necessary further complications of translating into money the cost of lives or injuries or loss of peasant working time). A cliometric analysis, in the strict sense, is therefore out of the question (and the possibility is even more remote for Greece than for Rome). However, an account based on a non-quantitative model remains both possible and worthwhile.

Here I can do no more than enumerate and describe the variables and point to some of the analytical problems, but first I must call attention to a major preliminary difficulty. No single topic occupies more attention in ancient history, more space in print, than the preliminaries leading to a war – the diplomacy, the steps leading to the decision-making, public attitudes and psychology. Yet it is neither mischievous nor perverse to suggest that there is no topic on which we are less well equipped to express any views at all. There is, for example, no defensible basis for such a statement as the following (chosen virtually at random from an infinite number of possibilities): 'There was still considerable feeling against the Persians at Athens and soon after the publication of this pamphlet (Isocrates' *On the Peace*) a popular agitation in favour of war with Persia led to a debate, in which Demosthenes spoke effectively for restraint in his speech *On the Symmories*. No responsible public figure could give any encouragement to this anti-Persian hysteria.'[29] All this rests exclusively on a few rhetorical remarks by Demosthenes himself, and one had better not ask for more detail or further nuances. How much anti-Persian feeling was there, and where was it located within the citizenry? Who made what specific proposals in the Assembly that Demosthenes succeeded in defeating (single-handedly, he later claimed, 15.6, though this was his first political speech)? Were there no 'irresponsible' public figures able and willing to sway the Athenian Assembly at that time?

It is a sobering thought that not only these questions are unanswerable but virtually all comparable questions are equally unanswerable for the whole of ancient history. We have precisely three collections of policy speeches on matters of war and peace, those of Demosthenes, of Isocrates (which were pamphlets rather than speeches) and of Cicero (for whom civil war was more commonly the issue rather than foreign conflict), and, after almost two centuries of scholarship, there is still no agreement about these advocates and their objectives.[30] How could there be, when the categories that historians compel themselves to grapple with are such as responsibility, honesty, sincerity, impartiality? It is doubtful that such personal qualities are important as historical factors, and it is certain that they are indeterminable in specific cases, whether that of Pericles or of Demosthenes or of the elder Cato or of any of the Scipios. Besides, the evidence consists of *ex parte* statements by the actors themselves with insufficient independent testimony to serve as a control. The ancient historian dare not forget for a moment that in this area his external witnesses are few and rarely either first-hand or reliable. What Cawkwell has written about Demosthenes offers a necessary caution in all cases: 'historical judgment need not follow what he said of himself and his opponents'.[31]

In short, even at the level of model construction, of making the essential simplifying assumptions, ancient wars can normally be examined concretely only after they have got under way. Even then, battles occupy much the largest part of the available, dubious documentation; remarkably little is known about problems of supply and logistics, of the economy generally in wartime or of morale unless a crisis occurred. Once a war came to an end, however, and particularly if there was a clear victory for one side or the other, the consequences lend themselves to the kind of analysis I am proposing. I am of course not suggesting that the consequences necessarily throw a better light, retrospectively, on either the causes or the conduct of a war, but I am satisfied that with respect to consequences we are in a better position to comprehend the place of warfare and of particular wars in ancient society.

The starting-point would be the profits in the narrow sense – booty (of which captives were normally the most valuable), indemnities and confiscated land. Some of these profits were immediate, as when a city was sacked, but some, at times in much greater amounts, were acquired afterwards, depending on the magnitude of the victory, the strength and social structure of the victor, and his objectives over a longer duration. Yet another differentiation has to be made according to the distribution of the profits, whether they went to individual soldiers, to commanders or to the state itself. Such distinctions were closely correlated with the duration of campaigns and their distance from the home base: the longer the time and the greater the distance, the more urgent was the need for income both for the state and for the troops. The two-year siege of Potidaea cost the Athenian state 2000 talents (Thucydides 2.70.2), but that was in the period when the imperial tribute was being used to build up large cash reserves, a rare practice among ancient states.[32] Even then, the prospect of a long absence from home raised the urgent question of finances, which meant, beyond extraordinary war-taxes, either profits from the enemy or levies on subjects or both. In his statement explaining why in the end everyone voted for the Sicilian expedition at the critical meeting of the Athenian assembly (6.24), Thucydides included the following: 'the great mass of the people, including those serving on the expedition, thought that they would earn money at the present and also add a force (to the empire) that would guarantee permanent pay in the future'.[33]

These are strong words, and they reflect what I believe to be the normal 'hand-to-mouth existence' of the soldier, whether citizen or mercenary, whenever military service took him away at a distance for longer periods of time.[34] Even the scale of preparation achieved by Athens for the invasion of Sicily did not suffice under those conditions, as events on the island in the subsequent two years showed. Eventually the critical test was always the availability of funds from subjects or from booty (or from both) and the prospects of foraging for supplies: by and large, ancient commissarial arrangements were necessarily most inadequate, soldiers were often hungry and they were regularly exploited by local or migratory merchants.[35] The importance of external sources of revenue was symbolized by the history of the *tributum*, the Roman extraordinary war-tax on property, levied when needed (which meant regularly during the Second Punic War), sometimes repaid from war profits, but finally abolished after 167 BC because subjects were then able to finance further Roman military ventures on any scale required.[36]

In time, financial considerations led to a fundamental change in the character of Greek and Roman armies, and a model must have a place for them. The citizen-militia of the late archaic and early classical periods was not replaced, because the military obligation of citizens, conscription, was not abolished, but it was in effect replaced in sufficient part by professional soldiers, whether more or less voluntary mercenaries among the Greeks or more or less conscripted *proletarii* in Republican Rome. The initial decision whether to fight or not, the attitudes of the troops, their behaviour, their demands all underwent change, whether we can detect it today or not. Correspondingly, so did the behaviour and role of their commanders, symbolized by their share in the profits of war. Uneven distribution of booty among officers and men, as in the Roman formula for the distribution of money to soldiers at triumphs in the early second century BC – centurions received twice as much as infantrymen, cavalrymen half as much again[37] – is a simple reflection of social hierarchy in the military sphere. No far-reaching consequences followed. What I have in mind is rather the development, which recurred in different forms several times in the course of ancient history, whereby military commanders obtained control of substantial financial resources and used them for personal political ends, for the seizure or the expansion or the stabilization of power. The tyrants of Sicily are perhaps the most continuing manifestation, from the sixth century to the end of Sicilian independence in the third century BC; the vast fortunes and the unparalleled power acquired by the major Roman commanders in the last century of the Republic – Sulla, Pompey, Julius Caesar, Octavian (Augustus) – are the most dramatic instances.[38]

That victory in war could lead to serious internal upheavals, economic, social, political, is of course a truism: one thinks immediately of the civil war in Corcyra and the oligarchic coups in Athens during the Peloponnesian War, and of the most far-reaching case of all, the replacement of the Roman Republic by the Principate. The question before us now is whether or not it is possible through the use of non-quantitative models to explain the presence or absence of such upheavals. I believe it is, but only after we have introduced into the models the factor of permanent conquest and empire. In antiquity, conquest regularly entailed the seizure of land for exploitation and the levying of fiscal or military burdens on the new subjects. This was a long continuing process in Italy, and the cumulative effect of the Roman system of occupying and exploiting great quantities of confiscated land, the *ager publicus*, was the 'proletarianization' of large numbers of peasants and the settlement of large numbers of veterans and other poor citizens at too great a distance from the city of Rome to facilitate (or often even to permit) their exercise of the rights and prerogatives of citizenship. The fifth-century Athenian empire, in contrast, though it also brought about the acquisition of extensive land-holdings among the richer citizens, little as we are able to concretize the situation, simultaneously shifted a relatively large fraction of the poorest citizens, perhaps ten thousand all told, to a higher census classification through the so-called cleruchy system.[39]

Here then are the rudiments of two different models of ancient empire: one a maritime empire, with limited opportunity for territorial expansion, relying on the navy and therefore compelled to give the common people, the *demos*, a dominant role in the political decision-making; the other a land-based empire, almost limitless in its capacity and its desire to expand, in which the ruling oligarchy retained both the major material benefits of conquest and unbroken political control. Both models, when properly worked out, would also contain an essential dynamic element. They would otherwise be incurably defective, for they would fail to suggest how and why the Athenian empire over-reached itself, whereas the Roman empire ultimately brought about a change in the internal equilibrium of forces so great as to destroy the Republic.

I remind you once again that it is inherent in model construction that there is a one-sided concentration on, an isolation of, certain factors to the neglect of others, relative or total. That is how to accomplish what Droysen proposed (as I have already quoted him): historians 'must know what they wish to seek; only then will they find something. One must question things correctly, then they give an answer.'[40] By starting with the profits of war and their distribution I hope to liberate us from the massive guessing-games that dominate the traditional accounts of ancient warfare, the supposed insights into the psychology and the thinking of the chief actors, into their knowledge, their assessment of the situation from day to day, and into public opinion, into the knowledge and the thinking of the popula- tion at large. Behind that approach there is a faith in the ancient literary sources that I do not share, an unshakable faith in their accuracy, honesty, reliability, good judgment, impartiality.

I illustrate briefly from a paragon of such an approach, Eduard Meyer's remarkable 38-page account of 'the outbreak of the Peloponnesian War' embedded in the long essay on Thucydides we have already considered.[41] His argument, crudely summa- rized, is that the prevailing view in Athens was that Pericles deliberately started the war by having the Megarian decrees voted – an argument that rests to an astonishing extent entirely on passages in the *Acharnians* (especially lines beginning at 515) and *Peace* (beginning at line 605) of Aristophanes and on what can be interpreted, from that starting-point, as implicit in wording that Thucydides attributed to Pericles;[42] that Thucydides' *History* is a powerful polemic against that view, but an indirect one because the historian's tactic was to play down the decrees rather than to combat the popular view openly; that Thucydides was correct in his judgment about the unimportance of the decrees as a cause of the war but wrong in failing to appreciate their impact on public opinion; that Thucydides' own preference (1.25) for growing Spartan fear of Athenian power as the 'truest cause' rests on a false assessment of Athenian strength; that it was in fact Corinth who forced the war; that Pericles did not actively desire the war but was prepared to accept that it should follow in consequence of his policies, none of which he was prepared to drop despite the risk of war; that Pericles saw what the mass of the Athenians were unable to see; that, in sum, Pericles' 'conduct was alone worthy of the Athenian power position and appropriate to the existing relations, in fact the only conduct that was statesmanly (*staatsmännisch*) possible' (p. 326).

This is a carefully constructed, coherent argument, based on impeccable knowledge of the ancient literature. Yet my reaction is one of complete scepticism. Meyer was writing exactly as if he were analysing German and European inter-state relations of the second half of the nineteenth century. The parallel between Pericles and Bismarck is drawn explicitly at one point (p. 302), and that is not all: we are also told that, though Athens was a nation of 'merchants and shopkeepers', she and the other Greek states could nevertheless have coexisted precisely like England and the rest of Europe in Meyer's own day, in 1899 (p. 312). Meyer was writing, furthermore, with full trust in the ability and reliability of a small number of ancient authorities from whom he drew his vision of the thinking of Pericles and of his intangible personal qualities, his impartiality, honesty, and so on, as well as the picture of Athenian public opinion, of what the mass of Athenians 'really' thought, believed, understood. I lack the capacity to read ancient minds and characters with such confidence. In my view, the chance that an account such as Meyer's bears any relationship to *wie es eigentlich gewesen* approaches zero. It is significant that no two historians who study the causes of the Peloponnesian (or any other) War in that way ever agree, yet they can all quote Thucydides and Aristophanes with equal facility.

As a minimum, my alternative approach would avoid importing into fifth-century BC Greece either Bismarck or England, the nation of shopkeepers. That would constitute an advance, though neither a great one nor a sufficient one. If the models I have pointed to – and that is all I can claim to have done – should prove useful when fully worked out and tested against the available evidence, I believe that the resulting narrative of the Peloponnesian War and its aftermath – which is the example I am ending on – would bear a closer relationship to reality than the existing traditional accounts. More than that one cannot ask of an ancient historian.

[6]

Max Weber and the Greek City-State[1]

In a subtle and very gloomy centenary essay, Heuss came to the conclusion that 'the special disciplines pertaining to antiquity have gone their way as if Max Weber had never lived'. This was the case despite the fact that Weber's *Agrarverhältnisse des Altertums*, in its 1909 version, was 'the most original, boldest and most vivid portrayal ever produced of the economic and social development of antiquity'.[2]

I concur with both judgments, and they remain too near the truth today despite certain developments of the past two decades. Heuss had remarked that his negative view was not contradicted by the parroting of certain Weberian notions in the scholarly literature, normally with neither understanding nor significance. That, too, could be further exemplified in the more recent discussions, but it is one sign of a change that such parroting has become more common in the professional literature because there has been a certain opening up of the study of ancient history to more theoretical, more sociological approaches. That seems to be particularly evident in countries in which the influence of (or at least the interest in) Marxism has been strongest. Characteristic of the most serious of these Marxist discussions is the following statement in the opening paragraph of Narducci's long article 'Max Weber fra antichità e mondo moderno': 'I personally continue to prefer the Marx of the proletarian revolution to the "Marx of the bourgeoisie"; but it is useless to conceal the fact that henceforth a creative renewal of Marxism cannot avoid a confrontation with one of its most lucid and acute critics.'[3]

I suppose it is not unreasonable to suggest that my own work has more than any other in recent decades provoked the discussion of Weber among ancient historians, first around my *Ancient*

Economy and more recently around my more overtly Weberian article on the consumer-city.[4] Some of that discussion has been dismissive, but some has been serious and that is a new phenomenon. The publication before the war of Hasebroek's two explicitly Weberian books failed to stir up any continuing discussion: the books were simply dismissed, occasionally with faint praise, in the context of the old debate between the so-called *oikos* theorists (Rodbertus and Bücher) and the 'modernists' led by Eduard Meyer and Beloch.[5] Even the few historians who acknowledged the contribution of Hasebroek failed to develop his approach further in their own work.[6] But today there is a genuine attempt to come to grips with Weber's image of the Graeco-Roman world and its development, even though that remains a minority interest in the profession.

This qualification deserves a brief exemplification. Thus, following a one-paragraph summary of the Bücher-Meyer controversy, Starr writes that 'this debate is absolutely meaningless, though dangerous'.[7] Or, my attempt to reopen a discussion of the concept of the ancient consumer-city (a concept developed by Bücher, Sombart and Weber) has invoked some indignant protests. Unfortunately, little of that criticism can be discussed seriously, since the bulk consists of a straight rejection (often accompanied by misunderstanding) of models in favour of traditional, positivistic cataloguing of discrete instances, one by one.[8]

However, this is not to suggest that ideal types in general and Weber's account of them in particular do not raise serious analytical problems. My interest here is in the latter, and it is necessary to stress at the outset that Weber himself never produced a 'fully unequivocal' account of ideal types, that 'there are firmly ascertainable variations between his earlier and his later writings, which he himself never discussed systematically'.[9] Fundamental philosophical problems arise,[10] but I restrict myself to a consideration of the way Weber deployed ideal types in his discussion of the Greek city-state and its politics. The consequence of my choice, I must affirm explicitly, is a far more negative tone, especially in the two final sections of this chapter, than would be the case with an overall assessment of Weber's work on classical antiquity. His analysis of the ancient economy and social structure is, as I have already indicated in agreement with Heuss, without parallel. But on Greek history and politics, he perplexingly offered no more than hints or faulty explanations. Even when his insights were sound, as with the critique of the traditional view of a tribal organization (with which I begin), he failed to develop them satisfactorily. Why this should have been the case is not clear, though I will suggest the direction in which explanations may lie, but my main concern is merely to register the situation. My subject is one of methodology in ancient history, after all, not Max Weber as such.

'Tribal Organization' and the City-State

No dogma is so pervasive about Greek history (or indeed Roman and 'Indo-European') as the one that there was a regular evolution from an early 'tribal' organization of society, based on kinship groups, to a political, territorial organization. The formulations and conceptions vary greatly, but in one form or another they are found across the whole spectrum of ancient historians for at least the past century and a half, ranging from Marxists under the immediate influence of Engels' *Origin of the Family* to such 'non-theoretical' writers as Georg Busolt to the more 'sociological' approach represented by Fustel de Coulanges and Gustave Glotz.[11] Here and there a rare voice of doubt has been raised, but without any lasting impact. Max Weber was not the first, but he was the most outspoken, to call attention to the fact that *phylai*, phratries, and so on were common in the city-states but unknown in those loosely organized Greek communities called *ethne*, which are conventionally held to have been 'tribally' organized.[12] The implications are staggering: we are left to believe the improbability that the evolutionary path proceeded from a kinship basis to a territorial basis, but that in those communities which failed to take that step the subordinate kinship-based units somehow disappeared.

Something is radically wrong with such a conception; yet hardly anyone paid much attention though it was impossible to contradict Weber's fundamental observation. We may note the morass into which Ehrenberg trapped himself within a few lines by trying to combine this observation with the traditional evolutionary view; or that Hasebroek, the most avowed Weberian among ancient historians, simply ignored the point and adopted the conventional view.[13] Weber himself was less decisive than usual: he returned to the problem more than once, but always briefly and sometimes hesitantly, as if he were unable to find the proper categories into which to fit the Greek kinship institutions once he had demolished the evolutionary scheme.

Only occasionally was there a voice raised in connection with a particular issue (not necessarily with any direct reference to Weber); for example, Cassola on the Ionian *phylai* or Andrewes on the single, anachronistic reference in Homer to the phratry as a unit of military organization.[14] But it was not until 1976 that a definitive study was published of the three pseudo-kinship groups in the Greek cities, the *genos*, the *phyle* and the phratry, confirming beyond question and expanding the Weberian insight.[15] The importance of Roussel's work was hailed by Gauthier in the *Revue historique*,[16] but, for reasons I cannot understand, it has failed to receive any other serious review (at least in so far as listings in the *Année philologique* to 1982 are concerned). That will not matter in the long run, since Roussel's destruction of the linear evolutionary approaches (specifically of the kinship-to-territory movement) is, in my judgment, unanswerable.

Neither Roussel nor anyone else would be so foolish as to deny the importance of kinship in the Greek world, in the *ethne* as much as in the *poleis*. However, that is not the issue; or rather, that is a false issue. *Genos*, *phyle* and phratry were not kinship groups in reality, whereas the nuclear family and in some circumstances the extended family were realities that retained great vitality everywhere in the Greek world throughout ancient history, in living conditions, in the administration and transmission of property, in politics. The place of the family was essentially unrelated to, and certainly independent of, the *genos*, *phyle* and phratry: that is the essential point to hold onto in any discussion of the subject.

It is also essential to remember that, apart perhaps from the Homeric poems, we have no evidence about the ways in which pre-state societies were organized in the Greek world. The habit of inferring from often outdated anthropological investigations of pre-state societies in Africa, Asia or the Americas fails precisely because those societies did not develop state-forms, and it is that development that concerns the Greek historian. If it was the case that membership in the Greek *polis* was normally acquired by inheritance, by a family-link, it does not follow that this was the only way of reproducing a political community in antiquity. The Romans, after all, admitted manumitted slaves to the citizen-body in large and increasing numbers in the later Republic and the first two centuries of the Empire. The descendants of these freedmen then became citizens in turn through inheritance, but that did not remove the 'oddity' of the initial mode of entry.

And it certainly does not follow that pseudo-kinship groups were the inevitable solution to the complexities of organizing or reproducing a territorial society. Nevertheless, as Weber wrote, 'the whole course of history shows . . . how very easily political community behaviour in particular generates the image of a "community of blood"'. Perhaps the neatest Greek example is the reorganization of the Athenian state machinery by Cleisthenes, 'structured altogether rationally and schematically', Weber wrote, yet 'it appears in the same sense as wholly ethnic. That does not mean that the Greek *polis* was in reality or in origin a tribal or lineage state (*ein Stammes- oder Geschlechterstaat*) as a rule; it was rather a symptom of the very low level of rationalization in Greek community life altogether.'[17]

Surely neither Cleisthenes nor any other thinking Athenian ever imagined that his new, artificial *phylai* were kinship-groups; yet they were given the look of a kinship-group, so to speak. There lies a major research problem in Greek history. The *origin* of pseudo-kinship-groups within the *polis* and of the major role of the family, nuclear or more extended, within the community is probably beyond us except in an abstract, speculative analysis.[18] However, there is rich and varied material from the Homeric poems on, which requires radical re-study once we have emancipated ourselves from the simple evolutionary scheme that has so far been pervasive.

How closely we remain tied to evolutionism is sufficiently revealed by the standard works on Greek family law, with their deep-seated belief in a single Greek concept of the family and family law despite the (to me) overwhelming evidence to the contrary.[19] A recent survey, entitled 'Kinship in Athens', contains the following in its first nine lines: 'Kinship relations . . . defined most of the significant rights, duties and sentiments of the individual . . . The descent groups, the tribe, phratry, clan, and *oikos*, were jural-political, corporate entities that determined citizenship, religion, and ownership of land. In each group members were assumed to descend from a common ancestor, whether or not actual genealogical links could be traced to him.'[20] These statements are each of them wrong in whole or in part. No one genuinely believed in common descent; these groups neither defined nor determined sentiments, property ownership or the other things they are given responsibility for; the state itself, which defined and determined much, almost disappears from sight.

Greek Demagogues and Domination (Herrschaft)

How does the Greek city-state fit into the Weberian scheme of *Herrschaft*? He himself never discussed that question properly: it was not an important concern when he wrote his *Agrarverhält-nisse*. In the end, rather surprisingly, he classified the Greek *polis* under charismatic *Herrschaft*, and that requires careful examination. The question of 'legitimate domination' preoccupied Weber in his last years. He returned to it several times, and we are left with a difficulty. There are variations in wording from version to version, and the relative chronology of the versions is not always obvious.[21] Nevertheless, certain points about the Greek *polis* remained essentially unaltered.

The *polis* was obviously neither a traditional nor a rational (i.e. bureaucratic) form of domination. That leaves only the charisma-tic type virtually by elimination, and it has to be said that the justification for that classification is extremely thin and casual. The key is the demagogue (*Führer*) and the form is a 'transitional' one, a 'plebiscitarian democracy', 'a type of charismatic domination concealed beneath the form of a legitimacy derived from the will of the ruled and continuing only through that'.[22] In a posthumously published essay there is a further and much stronger formulation of the charismatic principle: 'The charismatic politician – "demagogue" – is a product of the western city-state. In the city-state of Jerusalem he appeared only in religious garb, as prophet: the constitution of Athens, in contrast, was wholly geared to his existence after the innovations of Pericles and Ephialtes; without him the state machine could not have functioned for a moment . . . The manic fit of the Nordic "Berserker", the miracles and revelations of any hole-in-corner prophecy, the demagogic gifts of Cleon are for the sociologist as good "charisma" as the qualities of a Napoleon, Jesus, Pericles. The only point that is decisive for us is that they counted and functioned as charisma, that is to say, received recognition.'[23]

This is presumably a late text, and I do not know why Weber chose not to repeat these precise words in the copy of *Economy and Society* he had begun to prepare for publication. However, nothing in the latter suggests a withdrawal of anything I have just quoted. Serious problems and difficulties ensue. There is no need to repeat the well-known points that Weber's ideal types were never intended to be simple propositions about reality and that in his final years, precisely the period in which he was so concerned with the 'legitimate forms of domination', his account of ideal types and his analysis altogether had become extremely formal and 'unhistorical' (marked by changes in his language). But it is legitimate to ask whether Weber's assessment of the *polis* as a political organism departed so far from reality as to be unacceptable in any kind of discourse. I think it has, for several reasons.

1 – Everything we know about Greek history indicates that Athens was an exceptional *polis* (until it lost its independence in the third century BC), and that any attempt to generalize from Athens requires proper defence, which Weber does not offer. Presumably he would not claim any role for demagogues and

plebiscitary leadership in Sparta and possibly not in the oligarchic communities either, but he seems to have included within his model the numerous democracies of the fifth and fourth centuries BC, many of which were so small that I find it difficult to imagine the model in operation there. I say 'presumably' and 'seems' because there is nothing explicit in any text. There is only a possible implication in that direction from what is said in a few pages of the long piece on *The City* comparing Sparta with Rome and then going on to link Athens and the other democratic *poleis*. But that is very shaky ground from which to judge, especially since it is not certain that *The City* was meant by Weber himself to be linked to the account of domination, and since the concept of charisma as such is not mentioned there.[24]

There is a further difficulty created by Greek tyranny, a form of rule that was widespread in archaic Hellas and among the western Greeks all the time, and which became increasingly frequent again in the fourth century BC. Tyranny was apparently no problem for Weber: his insistence on a value-free conception of both legitimacy and domination meant that tyranny could also be (and indeed had to be) embraced within the three types of legitimate domination.[25] Beyond that, as Wolfgang Mommsen pointed out, Weber never considered 'possible types of "illegitimate domination" . . . In fact, one cannot escape the conclusion that in the context of Weber's sociological theory of "legitimate rule" there was no room for illegitimate forms of domination . . . A political system which is not legitimate in either of the three forms is, on the basis of Weber's conceptualization, bound to collapse at once, and conversely, any stable government, whatever it may be like, must be legitimate in some way or another.'[26]

2 – Even in Athens alone, furthermore, the demagogue in Weber's sense was far from omnipresent. He was absent in the period between Solon and Cleisthenes, his appearance was sporadic before the triumph of Pericles, and he is not easy to find between the death of Cleon and the final extinction of Athenian independence and democracy a century and a half later. This difficulty with the Weberian picture becomes most evident if we

ask who were the demagogues of the fourth century BC. The only name to which charisma can possibly be attached is Demosthenes, and his political career was so uneven, so full of failures as well as occasional successes, that he fails badly to pass the Weberian test. Otherwise there was no one who could reasonably have been considered in terms of charisma.

3 – Years ago I argued (and I believe that I demonstrated) that the position of an Athenian demagogue was an arduous one, full of tensions and virtually without respite.[27] Pericles did not finally attain his pre-eminent position until the ostracism of Thucydides son of Melesias in the early 440s, and he was deposed as *strategos* and heavily fined in 430/429. Cleon's career, little as we know it, included a defeat in the Mytilene debate of 427 and a far from spotless military record apart from his spectacular success at Pylos. And what could have been more inconsistent than the success record of Alcibiades? The persistent struggle required to maintain a position of leadership was consistent with Weber's conception, but I believe the latter to have no place for the possibility that a charismatic leader could lose his position and later regain it (even more than once). When that happened, I fail to apprehend the presence of genuine charisma, which Weber himself insisted was an emotional relationship, based on qualities that had nothing to do with the merits or demerits of a leader's programme or policies.

4 – Wolfgang Mommsen wrote that 'Weber stated quite bluntly that the people at large are, in fact, incapable of judging the political issues at stake on their real merits.' He then continued: the 'competitive struggle of various political leaders for the support of the people . . . is clearly the liberal model of competition which is transplanted by Weber from economics to the field of parliamentary mass democracy. With it goes the assumption that the eventual victor in this competition is not only likely to be the most qualified leader, in the formal sense, but also that his political programme is the best as well.'[28] I am unable to see the connection between the two halves of this formulation. How do the people who are incapable of judging the issues on their merits nevertheless choose in the contest for leadership a victor whose

political programme then turns out to be the best? Nor can I find any warrant for that in Weber's text.

A quarter of a century ago Wilhelm Hennis delivered a ferocious attack on Weber's types of domination in which he pointed out that 'they have nothing to do with the real quality of domination but relate only to the reflection, to the "motives for obedience" in the heads of the ruled . . . It has become a meaningless thing that can be placed in the service of any arbitrary goal.'[29] I myself can find no reasonable alternative interpretation of this particular section of Weber's work, nor to Hennis' further point that Weber marked a complete break from the long tradition of political theory that judged a state or regime by substantive norms, by the way in which it did or did not advance the 'good life' (in the terminology of the ancient Greek philosophers).

All this raises large questions about Weber's conception of *Herrschaft*. The current debate, stimulated particularly by Wolfgang Mommsen, is not new but it has been moved to a new level. In 1926 Otto Hintze had hailed the three types of legitimate domination as a 'brilliant discovery' that would transform historical study, whereas Otto Brunner dismissed the whole structure as unfruitful for historical research.[30] Political considerations were not much in evidence, until they were made central with the publication of Mommsen's *Max Weber und die deutsche Politik* in 1959. The reaction to this book was an angry one, especially on the part of those whom Mommsen has since referred to as the 'orthodox' Weberians.[31] Today, however, although there are still authors who continue to 'close their eyes to the serious problems involved in a theory of democracy that relies to a substantial degree on the concept of charisma',[32] there can no longer be much serious disagreement except over nuances, at least about Weber's contribution to what has come to be known as the elitist theory of democracy. His intellectual kinship with Pareto, Michels and Mosca, and his influence on Schumpeter, all pointed out by Mommsen, leave no reasonable doubt on this score.

The elitist theory, in a sentence, holds that mass apathy and non-participation not only characterize current democratic political behaviour but, more important, are absolutely necessary for the healthy functioning of democracy.[33] I have argued elsewhere that this view cannot be applied, as fact or as norm, to Athenian democracy,[34] and that restricted issue is my central concern here with the three types of legitimate domination.

I do not for a moment question the importance of Weber's 'discovery' of the role of charisma in politics, or the correctness of his claim that his three 'types' normally are to be found in combination, though I am less persuaded of the view that charisma is 'the main element providing a link between the three types of domination'.[35] I also appreciate the fear of all-embracing bureaucracy which lay behind Weber's ultimate championing of 'plebiscitary leadership-democracy', though I am unable to accept the safety-net he gave himself of calling plebiscitary democracy an 'anti-authoritarian' version of the charismatic principle of legitimacy because the ruler received the *formal* approval of the ruled. Weber himself removed the significance of formal approval when he immediately added that 'in fact the actual validity of the charismatic authority rests entirely on its acceptance by the ruled by virtue of their devotion to him (or confidence in him).'[36]

With respect to the Greek city-state, the critical question of fact is whether or not, as Weber firmly believed and expressly stated more than once, the competition among 'demagogues' for leadership was conducted solely in terms of 'emotional' appeals or in terms of programmes and policies. Again I must refer to my *Politics in the Ancient World* (published in 1983), in which I argued at length for the second alternative (without any direct confrontation with Weber). Greek writers about politics all thought that the 'demagogues' gained and maintained their authority through substantive promises, much as they may have disagreed on one point or another and much as the writers largely disapproved of both the demagogues and their promises. The evidence, as I read it, fully supports that view. How effectively promises were fulfilled is another matter: what counts is that the people expected results and at times, sometimes for long periods, felt satisfied with them. Otherwise the leadership fell. One may, if one prefers, express that in the loss of charisma, but my instrumental view of politics locates the explanation in the area of programmes and politics, not in the essentially mystical 'faith' which Weber stressed to the exclusion of other concerns.

It follows, if I am right about ancient Greece, that Weber's three forms of legitimate domination are flawed as a universal scheme in yet another respect. The Greek city-state was, to be sure, a rather curious and in a way ephemeral institution. And it may be that the form of direct democracy it took in Athens, in particular, was possible only when the numbers were as small as they were then. Nevertheless, a scheme that excludes the *polis* (and I believe Republican Rome as well) cannot claim universal validity.

The Problem of Greek Law

In his classic statement of the unique western quality of rationality in economic and political life, Weber included the law in a brief, almost self-evident assertion: 'Elsewhere there were lacking the strict juristic schemata and forms of thought of Roman law and of the western systems trained on it, essential for a rational doctrine of law, despite all the beginnings in India (the Mimamsa school), despite comprehensive codifications, especially in the Near East, and despite all Indian and other law books.' Modern industrial capitalism requires 'a calculable law and administration according to formal rules'.[37] This last, obvious point is repeated in various formulas throughout Weber's work; for instance, the 'growing need for experience and specialized knowledge on the part of the practitioner of law and thereby the stimulus to rationalization of the law in general have almost always come from the increasing importance of the exchange of goods'.[38]

Yet, the sociology of law, or at least the history of the law seen from a sociological viewpoint, turns out to be far from simple, and I am not persuaded that Weber succeeded in resolving major difficulties that he himself had perceived. I restrict myself to the case of ancient Greece. Greek law has been notoriously a stepchild in modern study.[39] Weber was no exception to the universal neglect of the subject. He had of course read the Attic orators, Plato and Aristotle, but he had neither made any independent

99

study of Greek law nor read the best available modern work on the subject.[40] Hence the long section on the sociology of law in his *Economy and Society* has only incidental remarks about Greek law and wholly fails to mention it at various main points, such as the law of pledge or of *epikleroi*, and most notably, in view of his stress on the importance of commerce in the later development of rationalism in law, the Athenian introduction of special courts for commercial cases. The contrast is striking with his precise know-ledge of the developments in Jewish law from the Hellenistic era to the period of the *gaonim*.

None of this would merit special notice were it not closely linked with Weber's image of the Greek city-state as a political structure. In the context of domination, unlike that of the sociol-ogy of law, Weber delivered a sharp, almost gnomic judgment of the law of the Greek city-state. Under the Periclean and post-Periclean democracy, 'trials were not decided, as in Rome . . . according to formal law, but according to "material" justice, in fact according to tears, flattery, demagogic invectives and jokes'. The only Roman parallel is to be found in Cicero's speeches in political trials. 'The consequence was the impossibility of the development of a *formal* law and a *formal* legal science in the Roman style.'[41] In its place we find the 'absolutely arbitrary *khadi*-justice of the popular courts', which 'endangered formal legal security so strongly that the continued existence of property is more surprising than the very severe reversals following every political failure.'[42]

Weber's personal psychology no doubt played a part in this denunciation. Nowhere were his German loyalties stronger than in his conviction that only the civil-law procedures derived from Roman law permitted a rational legal system.[43] There are astounding statements about the Anglo-American jury system that are not too far removed from the attack on the Athenian popular juries,[44] including the suggestions that the key lay in the guild structure of the English legal profession (which of course cannot explain the continued strength of the jury system in the United States) and that England, for a time the most advanced capitalist country, managed with its far from rational court system by 'an extensive refusal of justice to the economically weak'.[45] However, we may put aside these matters of personal psychology and examine whether Weber's view of the Athenian court system was correct, and how it dovetailed with his definition of the city-state as a fundamentally charismatic system of domination.

The one point about which there can be no dispute is that the Greeks failed to create a class of professional jurists or a body of juristic literature.[46] (The major philosophical literature about justice is something quite different.) Weber said rather casually that this was a consequence of the *khadi*-justice that characterized the Athenian court system,[47] but there are difficulties with that explanation. Not all Greek city-states had a court system like the Athenian, but they also showed no signs of a professional class of jurists or of a juristic literature. Nor, on his own account, did the Roman law of the Republic reveal a fully 'rational systematic character': that was the work of the late Roman, early Byzantine bureaucracy under absolute monarchs who ought to have reflected charismatic qualities.[48] Why these later emperors and their bureaucracies should have played that role is not obvious, nor is the explanation for the high development of legal rationalism in the Anglo-American sphere, despite the 'khadi-justice' element in the jury system and Weber's general denigration of the whole operation.

'*Khadi*-justice' is of course a typical Weberian coinage. Although he took the term from an Orientalist, Richard Schmidt, and stressed the religious overtones visible in its 'pure' form,[49] with King Solomon the paradigm (and today I should say that Hammurabi was not far behind),[50] he extended the concept to institutions that had nothing to do with *khadis* or *khadi*-like figures. The test was whether there were formal 'rational grounds for a [legal] judgment' or the decision was based on broader considerations, including notions of justice beyond the formal law.

I have indicated doubts about the explanatory value of Weber's extended concept of '*khadi*-justice' and now I must also express doubts about its application as a matter of fact to the Athenian popular courts. Weber's implied (but not cited) evidence consists of some of the forensic orations (though I have to stress that by no means all the surviving orations justify his sharp judgment) and some of the familiar anti-democratic literature, starting with the *Wasps* of Aristophanes. That is not unimpeachable evidence: how many legal systems can be judged from *ex parte* pleas for which we do not have even the arguments of the other side or the verdict as an indication, no matter how imperfect, of which views persuaded the jurors?[51] And there are warning-signs. Athenian political and commercial stability for two centuries is not really disputable, whatever some comic poet might say. It is hard to reconcile that with the picture of an irresponsible, irrational judicial system. There was also widespread agreement among contemporary writers that the hallmark of the genuine *polis* was rule by laws, not by men.[52]

Wolff and his pupils have argued, in support of the last point, that behind the conventional rhetoric of the forensic speeches there was an unfailing demand that the jurors enforce the laws (rather than an appeal to equity beyond the laws).[53] If this were true, it would be a powerful answer to Weber (who does not appear in any of this scholarly discussion). Unfortunately, matters are not so simple. It seems to have been largely overlooked that the statutes regularly failed to provide definitions. That has recently been demonstrated for the Athenian law of theft, and I long ago showed the same to be true in the non-criminal field of real security.[54]

It is worth considering whether this 'failing', as it would be considered by most modern jurists, followed automatically from the absence of a legal profession and a juristic literature, or whether it reflected a desire to prevent excessive formalization of the law, 'a resistance to the statism (*étatisation*) of justice'. Gernet used those words in his discussion of Athenian public arbitration, and it is the latter institution that warrants my suggestion of a deliberate 'openness' of the law.[55] Legal historians have not perhaps been sufficiently alert to the fact that most civil actions in Athens (and in other Greek city-states, though our information is too restricted) were preceded by more or less compulsory attempts at public or private arbitration.[56] Only when that failed was the dispute referred to a court, and it is in the nature of arbitration that it cannot simply 'enforce the law'. Aristotle put it sharply and clearly (*Rhetoric* 1374b20–22): 'an arbitrator looks to equity, a judge to the law, and arbitration was invented in order that equity might prevail'.[57]

The *polis* was a *koinon*, a community in the strict sense. That is the background of the tenacity of the old institution of arbitration long after a formal system of courts had been introduced. I may quote Gernet again: 'arbitration differs from justice in its narrow sense as a peace treaty differs from the application of an impersonal norm that is, with respect to the parties, transcendental. The first function of the arbitrator is to conciliate, to suggest concessions and to have them accepted. From one point of view, arbitration is violation of the "law" . . . Where one has a bone to pick with kinsmen or with neighbours, the "natural" society that one constitutes with them requires a more or less permanent equilibrium, the evaluation of which does not rest with an impersonal power.'[58]

Arbitration is not even mentioned in Weber's brief reference to Athenian judicial procedure. Of itself, that is not a great matter. However, it is one of too many points on which the conclusion imposes itself that his scheme of legitimate domination cannot cope with the Greek *polis*. In particular, the central role he assigned to charisma appears to be inappropriate. I can understand how '*khadi*-justice' with a *khadi*, a Hammurabi or a Solomon, is consistent with charismatic leadership, but not the Athenian demagogues or the Athenian judicial procedure. More study is called for, and it may be that the sources will in the end prevent a decisive formulation. But on present understanding the Weberian scheme is fatally defective. To dismiss the Greek *polis* in general and Athens in particular as irrational does not advance our understanding.

Epilogue

This short book is about fundamental problems of method in ancient history, and it is avowedly polemical in intention, concentrating on a small number of themes or propositions.

1 – The study of history (in which I include archaeology) is in no significant sense a science. That does not release the historian from the requirements of honesty in reporting, logical consistency in the analysis, and so on, but these are all secondary aspects of a scientific method without touching on the essential.

2 – The historian's evidence (whether documents, literary texts or objects) propounds no questions. Or, in so far as a literary text does ask questions, they are those of an individual author, not identical with those of anyone writing a historical account, that is to say, an analysis suitable to a later age. Therefore, the historian himself must ask the right questions (in the language of Droysen quoted two or three times in my text) and provide the right conceptual context. He must do that consciously and systematically, abandoning the stultifying fiction that it is the duty of the historian to be self-effacing, to permit 'things' to 'speak for themselves' (in Ranke's words).

3 – The long tradition, normally not expressed overtly but implied in the treatment, that sources written in Greek or Latin occupy a privileged status and are immune from the canons of judgment and criticism that are applied to all other documentation, is unwarranted and constitutes a major stumbling-block to any proper historical analysis. One example is the touching faith in the oral tradition of the Greeks and Romans, which no one shares who has to deal with oral traditions in other societies, and which does not stand up to scrutiny the moment other evidence is available. Defective sources cannot be 'rescued' by hard thinking alone, not even those written in the ancient classical language.

4 – The first questions to be asked of any written source are, why was it written? why was it 'published'?

All this goes against the prevailing tradition in the field. Very few ancient historians are introspective: one must infer their most fundamental presuppositions from their substantive accounts, since they refuse to discuss methodological questions. It is, I believe, correct to say that the prevailing tradition starts from the assumption that the text is 'sacred', that it is and must be the sole starting-point for any account or analysis. Therefore, to ask why a given text, or better, a given kind of text, was written and published is to move a giant step behind the text, to ask questions that the texts themselves do not pose and cannot answer directly. If we accept the proposition, as I believe we must, that what any given society asks or fails to ask, records or fails to record, by itself offers an important clue to the nature of that society, then my questions about why write, why publish, must be raised, and if possible answered.

At the eighth international epigraphical congress in Athens in 1982, D. M. Lewis noted that he was aware of fifty-two examples from Athens down to 321 BC in which an inscription recording a decree of the Assembly specified one or more amendments that had been made to the original proposal, whereas he knew of only nine instances from all the rest of the Greek world, and those, significantly enough, were from 'places which had heavy Athenian influence' (p. 61 of the Congress proceedings, published in 1984). That is a capital piece of information, previously unnoticed, and it warrants careful analysis of the implications for the history and functioning of ancient Greek democracy. Or to take another example: why was it that in Athens 'honorary decrees' for non-citizens were introduced a century before the practice was extended to citizens (in 346/5 BC according to the earliest known instance: Calabi Limentani in 3:20, p. 94). These may seem obvious questions, but they have been ignored because the traditional approach has failed to bring the essential data to the surface of consciousness. In his 1982 paper, entitled 'Democratic Institutions and their Diffusion', Lewis reported that 'the only major work I know in which the topic of the diffusion of

Athenian institutions is a principal theme is Swoboda's *Griechis-che Volksbeschlüsse* of 1890' (p. 55). That century of non-progress is enough to indicate how large a programme of work on the sources lies ahead of us, for the failure obviously lay not in a lack of interest in the diffusion of Athenian institutions but in the assessment and understanding of the available evidence.

These examples should also make it plain that my polemic is neither a purely negative one nor a counsel of despair. Nor is it a plea for one approach or method in preference to others. As I have argued several times, a historian must deploy different strategies according to the nature of the evidence available to him and the questions he is posing. Not even my stress on non-mathematical models is meant to imply an exclusive approach or procedure. As the experience of Max Weber in his final years showed, the deployment of models can become too abstract, too schematic. (Hence the negative tone of my final chapter, which may surprise readers as it surprised me by the time I had completed it.)

It is in the nature of a book such as this that it has to be largely restricted to pointers and objections. That is shown most fully in the chapter on inter-state relations, normally culminating in war, conquest and empire. Negatively, that chapter expresses my inability to accept the traditional accounts of ancient wars, based in the final analysis on guessing-games about the behaviour of individual leaders, about causes and motives, and so on. Tolstoi formulated the objections repeatedly in *War and Peace* better than I or any other historian has succeeded in doing. But at the same time my chapter also offers pointers to an alternative approach through models – only pointers, because, though I tried to indicate the main variables that need to be incorporated into a satisfactory model, I could not within such a short compass develop the suggestions into a full analysis. For that a large research programme is required, which, I am prepared to claim with considerable assurance, would produce an account of ancient inter-state relations such as we do not at present have, and would also transform for the better the 'histories' of the major conflicts, such as the Persian wars, the Peloponnesian War, the

Punic wars, or the growth of the Roman empire. By 'transform for the better' I mean produce an account that would come closer to 'how it really was'. More than that no one can legitimately claim; the severe limits to what we can possibly know about the ancient world can be pushed out a bit, even substantially, but they can never be broken.

Logically, of course, an analysis of the *polis* – Greek especially but also Etruscan/Italian and Carthaginian – has priority over the study of inter-state relations. That a radically new analysis is needed follows from my discussion of Weber's failure to locate the *polis* correctly. That may appear to be an odd suggestion, given the volume of writing on the subject since the late eighteenth century. But I believe that serious flaws in the traditional analysis can be discovered at two levels. One is the level of the structure (in the narrow sense) of the *polis*. I merely recall two aspects of the problem that I discussed in chapter 6, namely, the changing role of kinship organizations within the social and political system, and the nature of the legal system, including the judicial procedures. The latter has been discussed relatively little for Greece, endlessly in the case of Roman law but almost always in a purely formal way and not in terms of its location and role within the larger political and social structure of the societies in question. Two other aspects, most obvious ones, are economics and politics, and on both I have myself made a start in the formulation of models in *The Ancient Economy* (new ed., 1985) and in *Politics in the Ancient World* (1983).

The other level is the one Weber attempted, though rather fleetingly, and that is the location of the *polis* within a general typology of political structures. That the city-state was a particular and probably a unique kind of political organization is, at the least, a reasonable working hypothesis. Only the late mediaeval communes of Italy and northern Europe offer possible parallels, and it is notorious that neither mediaeval and Renaissance historians nor ancient historians have pursued the possibilities seriously. If, as I have argued, Weber's typology is inadequate to deal with the *polis*, if it fails to provide the essential elements for a model, what alternative schemes are available? I know of none, and I believe that to be a major need, not only for comparative purposes but also for a better and fuller understanding of the *polis* itself and of its history.

A third main topic has also been adumbrated in this book, namely, the ancient city as an urban structure (not to be confused with the *polis* as a political organism). Except for perhaps Athens and Rome, no ancient city is susceptible to a proper historical account, as I have tried to demonstrate. However, ancient urbanism is a fruitful topic, provided that models are properly deployed in order to avoid the familiar antiquarianism of endless enumeration of details, of 'tell all you know'. The models would have to be dynamic, so as to reveal the direction, the limits and the tempo of change, the important variations according to origin, period, political authority and so on. And so, too, do the other topics and areas I have indicated. The objective, in the final analysis, is the paradoxical one of achieving a more complex picture by the employment of simplifying models.

Notes

Numbers in brackets after titles refer to chapter and note where full citation may be found.

[1] 'Progress' in Historiography

1 – This introductory chapter is an extract, slightly revised, of my article, '"Progress" in Historiography', *Daedalus* 106 (Summer 1977) 125–42: 'Discoveries and Interpretations. Studies in Contemporary Scholarship'. Reprinted by kind permission of *Daedalus*, Journal of the American Academy of Arts and Sciences.

2 – Paul Veyne, *Comment on écrit l'histoire* (Paris 1971), p. 255.

3 – *Ibid.*, pp. 253 and 271, respectively.

4 – *Ibid.*, p. 267.

5 – Although I have sometimes changed my views from those I expressed in earlier publications on questions of methodology, I have not bothered to indicate the changes here. Throughout, unless otherwise indicated, my remarks do not refer to ancient historians, especially in the socialist countries, who accept Marxism as an overriding conceptual scheme.

6 – Martin Nilsson, *Greek Popular Religion* (New York 1940), pp. 4, 15 and 135, respectively. I have no reason to alter the criticisms I made in a review-article in *Studies in Philosophy and Social Science* 9 (1941) 502–10.

7 – Quoted from A. Momigliano's introduction to the Italian translation of the *Kulturgeschichte*, reprinted in his *Secondo Contributo alla storia degli studi classici* (Rome 1960), pp. 283–98, at p. 286*n*4, where other dismissive judgments are also cited.

8 – Karl Christ, *Vón Gibbon zu Rostovtzeff* (Darmstadt 1972), pp. 106–8.

9 – The phrase 'political pedagogy' is the title of chap. 3 of A. Wucher, *Theodor Mommsen. Geschichtschreibung und Politik* (Göttingen 1956).

10 – A. Momigliano, 'Ancient History and the Antiquarian', in his *Contributo alla storia degli studi classici* (Rome 1955), pp. 67–106, at p. 100 (originally published in *Journal of the Warburg and Courtauld Institutes* 13, 1950, 285–315).

11 – F. Millar, *The Emperor in the Roman World (31 BC–AD 337)* (London 1977), pp. xii–xiii.

[2] The Ancient Historian and his Sources

1 – A substantially shorter version of this chapter appeared in *Tria Corda. Scritti in onore di Arnaldo Momigliano*, ed. E. Gabba (Como 1983), pp. 201–14.

2 – 'Mesopotamian Social Organization: Archaeological and Philological Evidence', in *The Evolution of Social Systems*, ed. J. Friedman and M. J. Rowlands (London and Pittsburgh 1978), pp. 457–85, at p. 473.

3 – A. Momigliano, 'Ancient History and the Antiquarian' (1:10), p. 68.

4 – Herodotus 3.122; Thucydides 1.20–21.

5 – Thucydides' brief survey of Greek developments in the more distant past (1.2–18) is no exception: it is the expression of a general sociological theory about power and progress, not history in any usual sense.

6 – 'We do not find it too hard to recognize the inventive technique in comparatively unimportant details, but it does not come naturally to us to expect the *big* lie as well . . . Nowadays we have learned to pay lip-service, at least, to the dangers of accepting annalistic material as reliable, but the will to believe is still strong': T. P. Wiseman, *Clio's Cosmetics* (Leicester 1979), pp. 52–3.

7 – See D. Musti, *Tendenze nella storiografia romana e greca su Roma arcaica = Quaderni urbinati* 10 (Rome 1970).

8 – It is enough to cite T. J. Cornell, 'Aeneas and the Twins: the Development of the Roman Foundation Legend', *Proceedings of the Cambridge Philological Society*, n.s. 21 (1975) 1–32; E. Gabba, 'Storiografia greca e imperialismo romano (III–I sec. a.C.)', *Rivista storica italiana* 74 (1974) 625–42, 'Sulla valorizzazione politica della leggenda delle origini troiana di Roma . . .', in *I canali della propaganda nel mondo antico* (Milan 1976), pp. 84–101; C. B. R. Pelling, 'Plutarch's Adaptation of His Source-Material', *Journal of Hellenic Studies* 100 (1980) 123–40.

9 – R. M. Ogilvie, *A Commentary on Livy, Books 1–5* (Oxford 1965), p. 88.

10 – R. M. Ogilvie, *Early Rome and the Etruscans* (London 1976), pp. 174–6.

11 – F. W. Walbank, *Polybius* (Berkeley and London 1972), p. 44.

12 – F. E. Adcock, *Thucydides and His History* (Cambridge 1963), pp. 27–35. The lengths to which Thucydides continues to drive modern commentators is revealed in *The Speeches of Thucydides*, ed. P. A. Stadter (Chapel Hill 1973).

13 – J. H. Finley, Jr., *Thucydides* (Cambridge, Mass., 1942), p. 102. Or compare, on the speeches in Livy, that 'whilst one may regret that such speeches are unhistorical, in a literal sense, the psychological insight which they reflect' deserves nothing but praise: P. G. Walsh, *Livy* (Cambridge 1961), p. 220.

14 – See C. Schneider, *Information und Absicht bei Thukydides* (Göttingen 1974).

15 – It will be fairly obvious that I myself have no doubt that the speeches even in Thucydides are not authentic in any normal sense of that adjective, but I shall not argue the case further as my analysis would not fall because of an exception or two. I refer to H. Strasburger, 'Thukydides und die politische Selbstdarstellung der Athener', *Hermes* 86 (1958) 492–530, reprinted in his *Studien zur Alten Geschichte* (2 vols., Hildesheim and New York, 1982) II 676–708); Schneider, *Information*, pp. 137–54; briefly and cautiously, A. Andrewes and K. J. Dover, *A Historical Commentary on Thucydides*, Book VIII (Oxford 1981), pp. 393–9. *A fortiori* I have even less doubt about Polybius as the composer of the speeches in his work despite the heroic effort of Walbank to rank his authenticity as a speech reporter even higher than that of Thucydides: *Speeches in Greek Historians* (Third J. L. Myres Memorial Lecture, Oxford [1965]).

16 – Walbank, *Speeches*, pp. 18 and 2, respectively.

17 – It is worth noticing that today we tolerate, and even desire, much more leeway in these matters from biographers.

18 – *The Idea of History* (Oxford 1946), pp. 30–31.

19 – The great exception was ecclesiastical history from its invention by Eusebius early in the fourth century AD; see the subtle analysis by A Momigliano, 'Pagan and Christian Historiography in the Fourth Century AD', in *The Conflict between Paganism and Christianity in the Fourth Century*, ed. Momigliano (Oxford 1963), pp. 79–99, reprinted in his *Terzo Contributo* . . . (Rome 1966) I 87–109.

20 – See G. Klaffenbach, *Bemerkungen zum griechischen Urkundenwesen* (Deutsche Akad. d. Wiss. zu Berlin, Klasse für Sprachen . . ., *Sitzungsberichte*, 1960 no. 6), pt. 1.

21 – See chap. 3 below.

22 – F. Jacoby in *RE* XI 1617–21, reprinted in his *Griechische Historiker* (Stuttgart 1956), cols. 165–7. Despite such predecessors of Aristotle as the Sophist Hippias of Elis, it remains correct to identify the Peripatetics as the founders of Greek archival investigation.

23 – See the collection in *Fontes iuris Romani antejustiniani, Leges*, 2 ed., S. Riccobono (Florence 1941). Epigraphical finds since 1940 have not changed the picture significantly.

24 – For what follows, see Finley, 'Myth, Memory and History', *History and Theory* 4 (1965) 281–302, reprinted in my *Use and Abuse of History* (London and New York 1975), ch. 1.

25 – T. P. Wiseman, 'Legendary Genealogies in Late-Republican Rome', *Greece and Rome*, 2nd ser., 21 (1974) 153–64.

26 – Z. Yavetz, 'Forte an dolo principis (Tac. *Ann.* 15 38)', in *Studies . . . C. E. Stevens* (1975) 181–97. The grounds escape me for Yavetz's certainty that 'there must have been some basis for the contention that Nero set fire to the city'.

27 – A. Momigliano, 'The Origins of the Roman Republic', in his *Quinto contributo* . . . (Rome 1975), pp. 293–332, at p. 296.

28 – M. H. Crawford, 'The Early Roman Economy, 753–280 BC', in *Mélanges . . . Heurgon* (Paris 1976), pp. 197–207, at p. 198. He is writing specifically about early money and coinage but the characterization applies equally to other institutions.

29 – Wiseman, *Clio's Cosmetics* (2:5), p. 45.

30 – E. G. I^3 1, an Athenian decree regarding Salamis; the so-called *lapis niger* from the Forum: *Remains of Old Latin*, ed. E. H. Warmington, IV (*Loeb Classical Library* 1940), p. 242; the recently discovered inscription from Satricum: *Lapis Satricanus*, ed. C. M. Stibbe (*Arch. Studien van het Nederlands Inst. te Rome, Scripta Minora*, 5, 1980).

31 – Ogilvie, *Early Rome* (2:10), p. 29.

32 – Ogilvie, *Commentary* (2:9), p. 13.

33 – See, as a tentative beginning, comments in the two chapters by C. Ampolo and the subsequent discussion in the two issues of *Dialoghi di archeologia*, n.s. 2 (1980), on 'La formazione della città nel Lazio'.

34 – Inscriptions and papyri are not, properly speaking, archaeological sources; brick- and pottery-stamps are border-line.

35 – D. L. Clarke, *Analytical Archaeology* (London 1968), p. 13.

36 – See e.g. *Research and Theory in Current Archaeology*, ed. C. L. Redman (New York 1973).

37 – See e.g. B. D. Shaw, 'Archaeology and Knowledge: The History of the African Provinces of the Roman Empire', *Florilegium* 2 (1980) 28–60.

38 – John Boardman, in *Encounter* (April 1973) 67.

39 – See e.g. A. M. Snodgrass, 'La prospection archéologique en Grèce et dans le monde méditerranéen', *Annales, E.S.C.* 37 (1982) 800–12.

40 – 'In fact, it is or ought to be obvious that history is a single science, to which the different disciplines must contribute in their different ways and which in the final instance provides the ultimate criteria of assessment': F. Coarelli, 'Public Building in Rome between the Second Punic War and Sulla', *Papers of the British School at Rome* 45 (1977) 1–23, at pp. 1–2.

41 – T. Helen, *Organization of Roman Brick Production in the First and Second Centuries AD*, and P. Setälä, *Private Domini in Roman Brick Stamps of the Empire* (*Acta Instituti Romani Finlandiani* IX 1 and 2, 1975–77), with review by J. Andreau in *Annales, E.S.C.* 37 (1982) 920–5; Y. Garlan, 'Koukos', in *Thasiaca* (*Bulletin de correspondance hellénique*, Supp. 5, 1979), pp. 213–68.

42 – On the traps awaiting the historian, see J. Y. Empereur, 'Les anses des amphores timbrées et les amphores: aspects quantitatifs', *Bulletin de correspondance hellénique* 106 (1982) 219–33.

43 – See briefly J. Paterson, '"Salvation from the Sea": Amphoras and Trade in the Roman West', *Journal of Roman Studies* 72 (1982) 146–57, at p. 153, with bibliography.

44 – A. Tchernia, 'Quelques remarques sur le commerce du vin et les amphores', in *The Seaborne Commerce of Ancient Rome*, ed. J. H. D'Arms and E. C. Kopff (*Memoirs of the American Academy in Rome* 36, 1980), pp. 305–12; cf. A. Hesnard and C. Lemoine, Les amphores de Cécube et de Falerne, *Mélanges de l'école française de Rome. Antiquité* 93 (1981) 243–95, at pp. 262–4.

45 – P. A. Gianfrotta has made reference to such finds in *Bolletino d'Arte* 56 (1981) no. 10, pp. 80–81, and he proposes to publish a proper account shortly. These *dolia* have been found together with numerous Dressel 2–4 amphoras and are dated early in the reign of Augustus.

46 – See the short but important review by A. Drummond in *Journal of Roman Studies* 72 (1982) 177–9.

47 – J. C. Richard, *Les origines de la plèbe romaine* (*Bibliothèque des écoles françaises . . .* 232, 1973), p. xii.

48 – F. Coarelli, 'Topographie antique et idéologie moderne: le forum romain revisité', *Annales, E.S.C.* 37 (1982) 724–40, at p. 728.

49 – Cornell, 'Aeneas' (2:8), pp. 11–16.

50 – See above all A. Momigliano, 'How to Reconcile Greeks and Trojans', *Mededelingen* of the R. Dutch Acad. of Sci., n.s. 45 no. 9 (1982); cf. Cornell, 'Aeneas' (2:8); E. Gabba, 'Studi su Dionigio de Alicarnasso, I. La constituzione di Romolo', *Athenaeum*, n.s. 28 (1960) 175–225.

51 – See briefly T. J. Cornell in a discussion, *Dialoghi di archeologia*, n.s. 2 (1980) 206–7.

52 – See the historical chapters by H. S. Versnel in *Lapis Satricanus*, esp. pp. 102–7. Note should be taken of the suggestion by Stibbe (106n10) that the original name may not have been Satricum but e.g. Pometia, which has not been located.

53 – J. P. Morel, 'La céramique comme indice du commerce antique', in *Trade and Famine in Classical Antiquity*, ed. P. Garnsey and C. R. Whittaker (Cambridge Philological Society, Supp. vol. 8, 1983), sect. 3.1.1. This article (pp. 66–74) is an important statement of the methodological problems and principles.

54 – D. P. S. Peacock, *Pottery in the Roman World* (London 1982), p. 2.

55 – A good introduction is provided by Peacock, *ibid.*

56 – 'African Pottery', in *Trade in the Ancient Economy*, ed. P. Garnsey et al. (London and Berkeley 1983), pp. 145–62, at p. 155.

57 – See e.g. Morel, 'Céramique' (2:53); Morel, 'La produzione della ceramica campana: aspetti economici e sociali', and G. Pucci, 'La ceramica italica (terra sigillata)', in *Società romana e produzione schiavistica*, ed. A. Giardina and A. Schiavone (3 vols., Bari 1981) II 81–121.

58 – D. P. S. Peacock, 'Recent Discoveries of Roman Amphora Kilns in Italy', *Antiquaries Journal* 57 (1977) 262–9, with bibliography; cf. Hesnard and Lemaine in *Mélanges* (2:44).

59 – H. Cockle, 'Pottery Manufacture in Roman Egypt: a New Papyrus', *Journal of Roman Studies* 71 (1981) 87–95. Strictly speaking, only one of the papyri has been published; the others are mentioned in the article only in the case of variants. The two not published are for lease of one third and one fourth of a pottery, respectively, and one must assume, with the editor, that the remainders were leased in documents we no longer have. I have adjusted the figures accordingly.

60 – I have omitted some details and possible further complications. It is relevant for what follows immediately in the text that the practice has been known to historians for a long time, though not in such detail, from several other Egyptian pottery leases. Two, from the sixth century A D, are leases for a fraction of a pottery, one fourteenth in one case, one third in the other, for ten years and for the lessee's lifetime, respectively: *P. Lond.* III 994 (p. 259) and *P. Cairo Masp.* I 67110.

61 – Carandini, 'African Pottery' (2:56), pp. 156–8.

62 – In *Man, Settlement and Urbanism*, ed. P. J. Ucko et al. (London 1972), p. 950.

63 – Cited in my *Use and Abuse* (2:24), p. 88.

64 – C. Renfrew, *Problems in European Prehistory* (Cambridge 1979), p. 35.

65 – A. Guidi, 'Sulla prime fasi dell' urbanizzazione nel Lazio protostorico', *Opus*, 1 (1982) 279–85.

66 – See the reply to Guidi by C. Ampolo, and the ensuing discussion, in *Opus* 2 (1983) 425–48. That the definition of a city is far less simple than Guidi and his mentors believe is shown, e.g., by P. Wheatley, 'The Concept of Urbanism', in Ucko, *Man, Settlement* (2:62), pp. 601–37.

67 – Paterson, '"Salvation from the Sea"' (2:43), p. 157.

[3] Documents

1 – This chapter was originally written for a special number of *Annales, E.S.C.*, where it appeared in French in vol. 37 (1982) 697–713, and is reprinted by kind permission of the editors. It is by design restricted to documents as sources for the study of ancient economic history, but the essential points can be repeated for other topics in ancient history.

2 – The lecture was published in London in 1948 and was not reprinted in the posthumous collection of Jones's papers, *The Roman Economy*, ed. P. A. Brunt (Oxford 1974), on the ground that most of the substance (though not the introduction with which I am concerned) appears in later publications.

3 – A. H. M. Jones, 'Slavery in the Ancient World', *Economic History Review*, 2nd. ser., 9 (1956) 185–99, at p. 194, reprinted in *Slavery in Classical Antiquity*, ed. M. I. Finley (Cambridge, repr. 1964), p. 10.

4 – Slave prices known from the Egyptian papyri spoil the 'unity' and Jones excluded them for specious reasons. In the latest tabulation, 28 prices are available for the Roman period to the end of the second century A D, and a glance is sufficient to reveal not only that they do not fit the Jones pattern but also that they cannot be organized into any meaningful series: I. Biezunska-Malowist, *L'esclavage dans l'Egypte gréco-romaine* II (Polish Academy 1977), pp. 165–6.

5 – In commenting on this particular instance in *Ancient Slavery and Modern Ideology* (London and New York 1980), p. 129 and n.19, I gave the example of P. Anderson, *Passages from Antiquity to Feudalism* (London 1974), for repetition by a non-specialist on the *auctoritas* of a specialist. The practice is of course widespread; see e.g. J. Stengers, 'L'historien devant l'abondance statistique', *Revue de l'Institut de Sociologie* (1970) 427–58, at pp. 443–5.

6 – In *Faire de l'histoire*, ed. J. Le Goff and P. Nora (3 vols., Paris 1974) I 54.

7 – P. Vilar, 'Pour une meilleure compréhension entre économistes et historiens', *Revue historique* 233 (1965) 293–312.

8 – R. S. Schofield, 'The Geographical Distribution of Wealth in England, 1334–1649', in *Essays in Quantitative Economic History*, ed. R. Floud (Oxford 1974), pp. 79–106, originally published in *Economic History Review*, 2nd ser., 18 (1965) 483–510.

9 – *Ibid.* and E. J. Buckatzsch, 'The Geographical Distribution of Wealth in England, 1086–1843', *ibid.* 3 (1950) 180–202.

10 – The number of documents quoted in the literary sources, no matter how reliably or unreliably, would not significantly affect this summary account.

11 – See e.g. Demosthenes 57.

12 – P. Vidal-Naquet, *Le bordereau d'ensemencement dans l'Egypte ptolémaique* (Brussels 1967); J. Bingen, *Le Papyrus Revenue Laws – tradition grecque et adaptation hellénistique* (Rheinisch-Westfälische Akad. d. Wiss, *Vorträge* G 231, 1978).

13 – For what follows, see C. Préaux, *Les Grecs en Egypte d'après les archives de Zénon* (Brussels 1947). All previous publications on the Zenon papyri are now replaced by C. Orrieux, *Les papyrus de Zénon* (Paris 1983) and his forthcoming dissertation, *Les archives de Zénon. Recherches d'histoire sociale (Annales littéraires de l'Université de Besançon)*. Despite his persistent use of the word 'archive' and his reference to Zenon as an archivist, there is nothing in Orrieux's analysis that invalidates what follows in my account.

14 – Préaux, *Zénon*, pp. 31–2.

15 – *Ibid.*, p. 4.

16 – *Ibid.*, p. 31.

17 – I am neither arguing that the available documents are useless for the economic historian nor seeking to denigrate the positive results of many painstaking but limited studies. I am merely trying to indicate the limits we face: not even for the estate of Apollonius, let alone for the Ptolemaic élite as a whole, will it ever be possible to produce an account comparable to that section of Kula's study of feudal Poland that opens as follows (p. 122) – 'We know approximately what the Polish nobleman sold both on the microeconomic and on the macroeconomic level. We know this thanks to certain monographic studies on individual latifun-

dia and to the statistics on exports from Danzig': *An Economic Theory of the Feudal System* (London 1976; Polish original 1962).

18 – G. Mickwitz, 'Economic Rationalism in Graeco-Roman Agriculture', *English Historical Review* 52 (1937) 577–89.

19 – R. Duncan-Jones, *The Economy of the Roman Empire* (2nd ed., Cambridge 1982), ch. 2. In reviewing the book in *Gnomon* 49 (1977) 55–63, H. W. Pleket went to some pains to correct Duncan-Jones' 'corrections' of Columella, but that does not alter the position; it merely confirms my view that refined re-calculation of isolated single texts is a waste of time. A recent attempt by A. Carandini to 'rescue' Columella's calculations as a genuinely 'rational' procedure must be dismissed as fantasy: 'Columella's Vineyard and the Rationality of the Roman Economy', *Opus* 2 (1983) 177–204; see the brief critique in my *Ancient Economy* (2nd ed., London and Berkeley 1985), pp. 180–81.

20 – A sample is conveniently available in *Texts on the Economic History of the Greek World*, ed. H. W. Pleket, vol. 31 in the series *Textus minores* (Leiden 1964). Cf. the detailed discussion of another type of document by I. Calabi Limentani, 'Modalità della communicazione ufficiale in Atene. I decreti onorari', *Quaderni urbinati di cultura classica*, n.s. 16 (1984) 85–115.

21 – The source for Alexander's decree is Diodorus 18.8. Texts of the two inscriptions are available in *Dialectorum graecorum exempla epigraphica potiora*, ed. E. Schwyzer, nos. 620 (Mytilene) and 657 (Tegea).

22 – The text with the correct date appears in the 3rd ed. of Dittenberger's *Sylloge inscriptionum graecarum*, no. 364.

23 – Published with extensive commentary by W. K. Pritchett in *Hesperia* 22 (1953) 225–311; 25 (1956) 178–317; 30 (1961) 22–9.

24 – D. M. Lewis, 'After the Profanation of the Mysteries', in *Ancient Society and Institutions. Studies Presented to Victor Ehrenberg*, ed. E. Badian (Oxford 1966), pp. 177–91, at pp. 182–6. Nothing relevant to this discussion is added by the fragments of the inscribed stelae regarding public sale at auction in 402/1 BC of property confiscated from the Thirty Tyrants and their associates, published by M. Walbank in *Hesperia* 51 (1982) 74–98.

25 – Space prevents me from discussing the temple accounts, notably from Delphi, Delos and Epidaurus (mentioned briefly below), the best available examples of minute record-keeping.

26 – This has recently been noticed by C. Ampolo, 'Tra finanza e politica: carriera e affari del Signor Moirokles', *Rivista di filologia* 109 (1981) 187–204, at pp. 188–9.

27 – Lewis, 'After the Profanation', p. 187.

28 – *Ibid.*, pp. 188–9.

29 – M. Crosby, 'The Leases of the Laureion Mines', *Hesperia* 19 (1950) 189–312, with supplement, 26 (1957) 1–23. More *poletai* fragments are awaiting publication but Lewis informs me that they do not include fragments of mine leases.

30 – D. M. Lewis, 'Attic Manumissions', *Hesperia* 28 (1959) 208–38, with supplement, 37 (1968) 368–74.

31 – Klaffenbach, *Urkundenwesen* (2:20). Cf. for the specific case of Athenian honorary decrees Calabi Limentani, 'Communicazione' (3:20).

32 – For a recent example, see L. Canfora, 'Il soggetto passivo della polis classica', *Opus* 1 (1982) 33–51.

33 – See my *Studies in Land and Credit in Ancient Athens* (New Brunswick 1952; repr.

1985), summarized in 'Land, Debt and the Man of Property in Classical Athens', *Political Science Quarterly* 68 (1953) 249–68, reprinted in my *Economy and Society in Ancient Greece*, ed. B. D. Shaw and R. P. Saller (London 1981), ch. 4, with later bibliography, pp. 260–61. A study of *horoi* published since 1952 shows that the main conclusions have not been affected by the new documents: P. Millett, in *Opus* 1 (1982) 219–49, reprinted in the 1985 ed. of my book.

34 – See J. Andreau, *Les affaires de Monsieur Jucundus* (Ecole française de Rome 1974).

35 – *Ibid.*, p. 20.

36 – The analysis of the Jucundus archive is in fact severely limited precisely because the period is too short.

37 – Kula, *Feudal System (3:17)*, p. 181.

38 – For important examples of what can be done, see S. Lauffer, *Die Bergwerks-sklaven von Laureion* (2 ed., Wiesbaden 1979); A. Burford, *The Greek Temple Builders at Epidauros* (Liverpool 1969).

39 – C. Ampolo, 'Oikonomia', *Archeologia e storia antica* 1 (1979) 119–30, at p. 127.

[4] 'How it really was'

1 – This chapter was first published in German, under the title 'Wie es eigentlich gewesen', in *Historische Zeitschrift* 239 (1984), pp. 268–86.

2 – *The Papers of Christian Gauss*, ed. K. G. Jackson and H. Haydn (New York 1957), p. 293.

3 – *Historical Essays and Studies* (London 1907), p. 352.

4 – *Geschichten der romanischen and germanischen Völker*, 2 ed., reprinted in his *Sämmtliche Werke*, vol. 33 (Leipzig 1874), p. viii. Ranke repeated this statement more than once in more or less similar language, e.g. in the posthumously published introduction to a course of lectures of the early 1840s on German history: *Aus Werk und Nachlass*, ed. V. Dotterweich and W. P. Fuchs (Munich and Vienna 1975), p. 177.

5 – The evidence for Ranke himself is briefly but conveniently assembled by K. Repgen, 'Über Rankes Diktum von 1824 . . .', *Historisches Jahrbuch* 102 (1982) 439–49, at pp. 445–9, who made the discovery that 'how it really was' is a direct quotation, hitherto unnoticed, of Thucydides 2.48.3.

6 – H. Holborn, *History and the Humanities* (Garden City, N.Y., 1972), p. 91.

7 – The phrase is Holborn's, *ibid.*, p. 36.

8 – It went through eight editions in his own lifetime, the first in 1838, the last in 1885, some of them with substantial revisions and supplements, so that the work finally closed with the Vatican Council of 1869–70.

9 – As early as 1824, before he thought to turn to the archives, he published, as a supplementary volume to his first book (on the Latin and Germanic states between 1494 and 1514), a remarkable, detailed analysis of the reliability of *published* historical accounts in Italian, French, German and Spanish: *Zur Kritik neuerer Geschichtschreiber* (Leipzig and Berlin). This book, reprinted in his *Sämmt-liche Werks*, 2 ed., vol. 34 (Leipzig 1874), is arguably much more important than the history itself: see E. Schulin, 'Rankes erstes Buch', *Historische Zeitschrift* 203 (1966) 581–609, at pp. 588–9. The first and much the longest chapter demolished the paragon, Guicciardini, on every count, including the fictitiousness of the

speeches in his work. Given the parallel with the speeches in Thucydides, it is interesting that Ranke concluded with the following judgment: 'One must concede that these *discorsi* in Guicciardini are something truly original, full of spirit and penetration.' They 'are not only a presentation of Guicciardini's mind alone; they rest . . . only too well on the situation in his native city of Florence.' There lies 'the merit of his work' (pp. 47–8).

10 – B. Croce, *History as the Story of Liberty*, trans. S. Sprigge (Meridian Books ed., 1955), p. 89.

11 – On Heine and Burckhardt, see Croce, *ibid.*, pp. 80–103; on Droysen, B. Bravo, *Philologie, histoire, philosophie de l'histoire, Étude sur J. G. Droysen*, (Polish Acad. of Sciences 1968), pp. 285–8, 305–10.

12 – F. Meinecke, *Ranke und Burckhardt* (Berlin 1948), reprinted in an English translation by H. H. Rowen in *German History*, ed. Hans Kohn (London 1954), ch. 7, where the quotation appears on p. 143. Cf. the review-article by E. Kessel, 'Ranke und Burckhardt', *Archiv für Kulturgeschichte* 33 (1951) 351–79.

13 – Letter to Arendt, 18 May 1846, quoted from Bravo, *Droysen*, p. 286.

14 – *Sämmtliche Werke* 16 (Leipzig 1877), p. 103; 21 (1879), p. 114.

15 – Probably the most detailed attempt to thread through Ranke's oeuvre with this problem in mind is L. Krieger, *Ranke: The Meaning of History* (Chicago 1977). Chapter headings such as 'The Unscientific Counterpoint', 'The Incomplete Historian', 'The First Synthesis' (and the second and third) point to the difficulties, as do such categories of explanation as 'fruitful ambiguity'.

16 – Quoted in H. Butterfield, *Man on His Past* (Cambridge 1955), pp. 219 and 221.

17 – The words quoted are taken from a Venetian manuscript in the Vienna archives, quoted at greater length by Ranke in a footnote.

18 – *The History of the Popes*, rev. trans. by G. R. Dennis (3 vols., London 1908) I 391, 393 = 7th ed. in *Sämmtliche Werke* 37, pp. 320, 321.

19 – Krieger, *Ranke*, p. 157.

20 – English I 464; German XXXVIII 45.

21 – Quoted from Butterfield, *Man on His Past*, p. 222.

22 – J. G. Droysen, *Historik*, ed. R. Hübner (Darmstadt 1958), pp. 35–6.

23 – *Geschichte des Altertums* I 1 (6 ed., Darmstadt 1953); 'Zur Theorie und Methodik der Geschichte', in his *Kleine Schriften* (2 ed., Halle 1924) I 1–61; 'Thukydides', in his *Forschungen zur Alten Geschichte* II (Halle 1899), pp. 269–436. On Thucydides and Ranke, see *Geschichte*, p. 211.

24 – See A. Momigliano, 'Premesse per una discussione su Eduard Meyer', *Rivista storica italiana*, 93 (1981) 384–98; Christ, *Von Gibbon* (1:8), ch. 11; on his political role, L. Canfora, *Intellettuali in Germania* (Bari 1979).

25 – Weber, *Gesammelte Aufsätze zur Wissenschaftslehre* (5 ed., Tübingen 1982), pp. 215–90, at p. 265. (I have adapted the English translation by E. A. Shils and H. A. Finch, in their ed. called *The Methodology of the Social Sciences*, Glencoe, Ill., 1949, where the quotation appears on p. 163.) It is characteristic of Meyer that when he reprinted his essay on the theory and method of history, he made two trivial acknowledgements of the objections raised by Weber in his 'full' and 'commendable' criticism but refused to alter his text. I pointed out in *Ancient Slavery and Modern Ideology* (London and New York 1980), p. 195n94, that Meyer had done exactly the same with Weber's critique of his *Wirtschaftliche Entwicklung des Altertums*.

26 – *Kleine Schriften*, p. 3.

27 – *Ibid.*, p. 28, cf. p. 16; *Geschichte*, pp. 185–6.

28 – *Forschungen*, p. 378, cf. p. 287.

29 – *Ibid.*, pp. 380, 386. The account of the speeches in Thucydides occupies pp. 380–400.

30 – See the opening of my 'Myth, Memory' (2:24).

31 – *Gesammelte Schriften*, vol. 4, ed. A. Leitzmann (Berlin 1905), pp. 35–56, at pp. 35–6 (in the English translation published in *History and Theory* 6, 1967, 57–71, at pp. 57–8).

32 – Droysen, *Historik*, pp. 324 and 422, respectively. In our own day, Hayden White, who certainly does not underestimate Humboldt's importance, has said of the 1821 essay: 'only the most generous critic could concede to this argument any claim to the rigour that a genuine philosophical analysis ought to display': *Metahistory* (Baltimore and London 1973), p. 182.

33 – E. Guglia, *Leopold von Rankes Leben und Werken* (Leipzig 1893), p. 54. This is a thorough and reliable work, and I have not attempted to check the assertion in the vast Ranke corpus, other than in the two volumes of letters published posthumously in 1939 and the four-volume *Nachlass* published in 1964–75.

34 – (Middletown, Conn., 1968).

35 – See Iggers, *ibid.*, pp. 63–5.

36 – In his edition of Manilius I (2nd ed., 1937), p. 87.

37 – Holborn, *History* (4:6), p. 83.

38 – C. N. Cochrane, *Thucydides and the Science of History* (London 1929), p. 26.

39 – Adam Parry, 'The Language of Thucydides' Description of the Plague', *Bulletin of the London Institute of Classical Studies* 16 (1969) 106–18, at p. 113.

40 – P. Gardiner, *The Nature of Historical Explanation* (Oxford 1952), pp. 60–61.

41 – I. Berlin, 'The Concept of Scientific History', in his *Concepts and Categories*, ed. H. Hardy (London 1978), pp. 103–42, at pp. 126–9 (originally published in *History and Theory* 1, 1960, 1–31).

42 – W. G. Runciman, *Sociology in Its Place* (Cambridge 1970), p. 10; cf. the review-article by P. Abrams, 'Sociology and History', *Past & Present* 52 (1971) 118–25. For a detailed defence of the position that the differences between the natural and the social sciences (including history) are essentially only technical, see W. G. Runciman, *A Treatise on Social Theory* I (Cambridge 1983).

43 – See e.g. R. W. Fogel, '"Scientific" History and Traditional History', in *Which Road to the Past?*, by Fogel and G. R. Elton (New Haven and London 1983), pp. 7–70 (originally published in *Logic, Methodology and Philosophy of Science* 6, 1982, 15–61). The case is argued at length in E. Leroy Ladurie, *Le territoire de l'historien* (2 vols., Paris 1973–8).

44 – *Ibid.*, p. 26.

45 – Berlin, 'Scientific history', pp. 118–9.

46 – Finley, 'Progress' (1:1), p. 139.

47 – Fogel, '"Scientific" History', p. 48.

48 – Fogel, *ibid.*, pp. 67–9.

49 – See L. Stone, 'The Revival of Narrative: Reflections on a New Old History', *Past & Present* 85 (1979) 3–24, with rejoinders by E. J. Hobsbawm and P. Abrams, in *ibid.* 86 (1980) 3–8 and 87 (1980) 3–16, respectively.

50 – M. Mandelbaum, 'A Note on History as Narrative', *History and Theory* 6 (1967) 413–9, at p. 417.

51 – Fogel, '"Scientific" History', pp. 69–70.

52 – As an indicator of the range of possibilities, see the chapters by A. M. Snodgrass, Y. Garlan, C. Goudineau, A. Tchernia, G. Pucci and A. Carandini, in Garnsey, *Trade* (2:56); or S. C. Humphreys, 'Family Tombs and Tomb-Cult in Classical Athens', in her *The Family, Women and Death* (London 1983), ch. 5, originally published in *Journal of Hellenic Studies* 100 (1980) 96–126.

53 – *Socio-Economic Models in Geography*, ed. R. J. Chorley and P. Haggett (abridged paperback ed., London 1968), p. 22. For an account by a Marxist economic historian, see Kula, *Feudal System* (3.17), ch. 2.

54 – Weber, *Wissenschaftslehre* (4:25), p. 191 (English, p. 90). That there are difficulties with Weber's own deployment of ideal types, especially towards the end of his life, is a separate problem; see chap. 6 below, with respect to the Greek city-state.

55 – J. Beloch, *Die Bevölkerung der griechisch-römischen Welt* (Leipzig 1886, repr. New York 1979), p. 259.

56 – Fraser, *Alexandria*, I 91 and the long note 358.

57 – For this and for what follows immediately, see E. A. Wrigley, 'A Simple Model of London's Importance in Changing English Society and Economy, 1650–1750', in *Towns in Societies*, ed. P. Abrams and Wrigley (Cambridge 1978), pp. 215–43.

58 – See A. Jähne, 'Die *Alexandreon Chora*', *Klio* 63 (1981) 63–103, and, more generally, P. Briant, 'Colonisation hellénistique et populations indigènes. . .', *Klio* 60 (1978) 57–92.

59 – E. T. Salmon, *Samnium and the Samnites* (Cambridge 1967), p. 50.

60 – G. Alföldy, *Noricum*, trans. A. Birley (London and Boston 1974), p. 43.

61 – Weber, *Wissenschaftslehre* (4:25), p. 195 (English, p. 94).

62 – J. V. A. Fine, *Horoi* (Hesperia, Suppl. 9, 1951), pp. v–vi.

[5] War and Empire

1 – Published in German in *Historische Zeitschrift* 259 (1984), 286–308, and in Italian, abridged, in *Prometeo* (Dec. 1984) 72–9.

2 – The extraordinary denial of this proposition by W. Nestle, *Der Friedensgedanke in der antiken Welt* (Philologus, Supp. 30.1, 1938) is in flagrant contradiction with his own text and it confuses the facts about war in antiquity with a selection of ancient value-judgments about the morality of warfare.

3 – M. Launey, *Recherches sur les armées hellénistiques* (2 vols., Bibl. des Ecoles françaises . . . 169, 1949–50) II 1087.

4 – The two calculations mentioned are by P. A. Brunt, *Italian Manpower 225 BC–AD 14* (Oxford 1971), pt. IV, and K. Hopkins, *Conquerors and Slaves* (Cambridge 1978), pp. 32–5, respectively. The sources are recognized to be a complete mess, but attacks on the way Brunt has dealt with them seem to me not to touch in any serious way the point with which I am concerned, e.g. F. Gschnitzer, 'Das System der römischen Heeresbildung im Zweiten Punischen Krieg . . .', *Hermes* 109 (1981) 59–85.

5 – *Weltgeschichtliche Betrachtungen*, in the edition of Burckhardt's collected works

published in Basel and Stuttgart, vol. 4 (1978), pp. 118–19. Cf. the ancient testimonia assembled by H. Fuchs, 'Der Friede als Gefahr – Der Zweiten Einsiedler Hirtengedicht', *Harvard Studies in Classical Philology* 63 (1958) 363–85.

6 – A. Momigliano, 'Some Observations on Causes of War in Ancient Historiography', in his *Secondo Contributo* . . . (Rome 1960), pp. 13–28, and again in his *Studies in Historiography* (London 1966), ch. 7; cf. the introduction to Y. Garlan, *War in the Ancient World*, trans. by J. Lloyd (London 1975). The latter notes (p. 17) that 'war never provided the title or subject of a single ancient philosophical treatise'.

7 – Momigliano, *ibid.*, pp. 19–21.

8 – E. B. McNeil, ed., *The Nature of Human Conflict* (Englewood Cliffs, N. J., 1945), pp. 27–8, quoted by J. R. Hale, 'Sixteenth-Century Explanations of War and Violence', *Past & Present* 51 (1971) 3–36, at p. 7n7, who adds that the 'situation has not significantly changed since 1945'.

9 – On the psychological implications of gladiatorial shows, see K. Hopkins, *Death and Renewal* (Cambridge 1983), ch. 1; on 'piracy', see above all Y. Garlan, 'Signification historique de la piraterie grecque', *Dialogues d'histoire ancienne* 4 (1978) 1–16, and, in a specific case, R. Brulé, *La piraterie crétoise hellénistique* (*Annales* . . . *Besançon* 27, 1978).

10 – I regret that I am not persuaded by the much more positive evaluation of Delbrück's work in Christ, *Von Gibbon* (1:8), ch. 8.

11 – See Y. Garlan, 'Eléments de polémologie marxiste', in *Mélanges* . . . *Daux* (Paris 1974), pp. 139–45.

12 – Marx, *Grundrisse*, in the translation by J. Cohen of the section called *Precapitalist Economic Formations* (London 1964), p. 89; see the complete Penguin ed. p. 491 (cf. p. 474).

13 – P. Anderson, *Passages from Antiquity to Feudalism* (London 1974), pp. 28 and 62, respectively.

14 – See Brunt, *Manpower*; Hopkins, *Conquerors*, ch. 1; W. V. Harris, *War and Imperialism in Republican Rome* (Oxford 1979), ch. 2; and already M. Weber, 'Die Agrarverhältnisse im Altertum', in his *Gesammelte Aufsätze zur Sozial–und Wirtschaftsgeschichte* (Tübingen 1924), pp. 1–288, at pp. 271–8.

15 – *La guerra e la pace nel mondo antico* (Turin 1901), p. 152.

16 – The De Sanctis attack was published together with the appendix in his *Per la scienza dell' antichità* (Turin 1909), pp. 231–99, the whole of which was then republished in his *Scritti minori*, ed. A. Ferrabino and S. Accame (Rome 1972), where the relevant pages are 203–49. In introducing the volume, De Sanctis called it 'un libro de battaglia'. The Croce reference is *Storia della storiografia italiana nel secolo decimonono* (2 vols., Bari 1921) II 233–5. See L. Polverini in *Annali* . . . *Pisa*, 3rd. ser., 3 (1973) 1071–5.

17 – The fullest text is Justin 9.1–20; for other references, going back to the contemporary historian Theopompus, and a detailed analysis, see A. Momigliano. 'Della spedizione scitica de Filippo alla spedizione scitica di Dario', *Athenaeum*, n.s. 11 (1933) 336–59, reprinted in his *Quinto Contributo* . . . (2 vols., Rome 1975), pp. 485–510.

18 – Harris, *War*, p. 74.

19 – I follow Aymard in preferring the neutral word 'profits' to the more pejorative 'booty' (or worse still, 'loot'), because the former more accurately describes the reality, which included not only money and other movables but also captives, all

taken on the spot, and sometimes large indemnities and territory taken in the final settlement: A. Aymard, 'Le partage des profits de la guerre dans les traités d'alliance antiques', *Revue historique* 217 (1957) 233–49, reprinted in his *Etudes d'histoire ancienne* (Paris 1967), pp. 499–512. See further in *Armées et fiscalité dans le monde antique* (Paris, CNRS 1977) the articles by Garlan (149–64) and Ducrey (421–34), and also P. Ducrey, *Le traitement des prisonniers de guerre dans le monde antique* (Paris 1968), ch. 7.

20 – W. K. Pritchett, *The Greek State at War*, vol. 1 (Berkeley 1971), p. 53. The statement still holds, though there has been more interest in the topic in the past decade.

21 – See the bibliography cited in n. 19.

22 – E. Gruen, in a review in *Journal of Interdisciplinary History* IV 2 (1973) 274.

23 – E.g. the 'League of Delos was founded because of a dispute about booty and its purpose was to get more booty': R. Sealey, 'The Origin of the Delian League', in *Ancient Society and Institutions, Studies . . . Victor Ehrenberg*, ed. E. Badian (Oxford 1966), pp. 233–55, at p. 253. Contra: K. Raaflaub, 'Beute, Vergeltung, Freiheit? Zur Zielsetzung des Delisch-Attischen Seebundes', *Chiron* 9 (1979) 1–22; A. H. Jackson, 'The Original Purpose of the Delian League', *Historia* 18 (1969) 12–16. Commercial rivalry, another favourite in some quarters, has no more to be said for it.

24 – Q. Wright, *A Study of War* (2 vols., Chicago 1942) I 220–1, 239.

25 – M. Amit, *Great and Small Poleis* (Brussels 1973), pp. 7–8.

26 – G. E. M. de Ste. Croix, *The Origins of the Peloponnesian War* (London 1972), pp. 213–20.

27 – See Finley, 'Empire in the Graeco-Roman World', *Greece & Rome*, n.s. 25 (1978) 1–15 (with bibliography). A major blow to the absence-of-mind doctrine has been struck by Harris, *War*; for a rearguard defensive action, see the review of the book by A. N. Sherwin-White, in *Journal of Roman Studies* 80 (1980) 177–81.

28 – See de Ste. Croix, *ibid.*, pp. 34–43.

29 – T. T. B. Ryder, *Koine Eirene* (Oxford 1965), p. 92.

30 – A convenient conspectus on Demosthenes and Isocrates is provided by the collection of articles in S. Perlman, ed., *Philip and Athens* (Cambridge and New York 1973).

31 – G. Cawkwell, *Philip of Macedon* (London and Boston 1978), p. 19. Cf. on the speeches of Cicero: 'He championed unworthy causes for short-term results in front of audiences that he despised. He turned on spurious emotion so often that it is difficult to know when he is sincere. He used his outstanding talents to frustrate rather than to promote action': R. G. M. Nisbet, in *Cicero*, ed. T. A. Dorey (London 1969), p. 78.

32 – Lump payments from the reserve explain why Thucydides was able to report a total figure; contrast his inability (6.31) even to guess at the costs of the Sicilian expedition.

33 – The translation is uncertain and the whole passage is a model of confusion and unintelligibility. Nevertheless, what I write immediately below is a reasonable consequence of any likely interpretation of Thucydides' words.

34 – The words quoted come from Pritchett, *War* (5:20) I 29. He was writing specifically about Greek armies of the fourth and third centuries BC, but the difference from earlier (or later, including Roman) armies was not one of period

but of the increasing practice of fighting wars at greater distances and of longer duration.

35 – On pay and supplies, see Pritchett, *ibid.*, ch. 1–2; Garlan, *War* (5:6), pp. 134–45; C. Nicolet, *Le métier de citoyen dans la Rome républicaine* (Paris 1976), pp. 156–66.

36 – See C. Nicolet, *Tributum* (Bonn 1976).

37 – See the table in Brunt, *Manpower*, p. 394, reprinted in Nicolet, *Métier*, pp. 163–4.

38 – I. Shatzman, 'The Roman General's Authority over Booty', *Historia* 21 (1972) 177–205, is important despite the narrow legal problem he set himself.

39 – A. H. M. Jones, *Athenian Democracy* (Oxford 1957), pp. 167–76.

40 – Droysen, *Historik* (4:22), pp. 35–6.

41 – Meyer, *Forschungen* (4:23) II 296–333.

42 – It is a desperate measure to drag in the short phrase of Andocides 3.8, 'going to war because of the Megarians', when all the 'history' in that oration is notoriously inaccurate.

[6] Max Weber and the Greek City-State

1 – This is a somewhat altered version of a paper presented at the special Max Weber section of the 16th International Historical Congress in Stuttgart on 25 August 1985.

2 – A. Heuss, 'Max Webers Bedeutung für die Geschichte des griechisch-römischen Altertums', *Historische Zeitschrift* 201 (1965) 529–56, at pp. 554 and 538, respectively.

3 – *Quaderni di storia* 14 (1981) 31–77.

4 – Finley, *The Ancient Economy* (Berkeley and London 1973; 2 ed., 1985); 'The Ancient City: from Fustel de Coulanges to Max Weber and beyond', *Comparative Studies in Society and History* 19 (1977) 305–27, reprinted in my *Economy and Society in Ancient Greece*, ed. B. D. Shaw and R. P. Saller (London and New York 1982), ch. 1.

5 – J. Hasebroek, *Staat und Handel im alten Griechenland* (Tübingen 1928; English trans., London 1933), *Griechische Wirtschafts- und Gesellschaftsgeschichte bis zur Perserzeit* (Tübingen 1931); see Finley, 'Classical Greece', in *Proceedings* of the 2nd International Conference in Economic History 1962 (Paris and The Hague 1965; repr. New York 1979), pp. 11–35; E. Will, 'Trois quarts de siècle de recherches sur l'économie grecque', *Annales, E.S.C.* 9 (1954) 7–22. The main papers in the so-called *oikos* controversy were reprinted in Finley, ed., *The Bücher-Meyer Controversy* (New York 1979).

6 – A good example is that of Helmut Berve; see his *Griechische Geschichte*, vol. 1 (Freiburg 1931), p. 128, in contrast to the complete silence in his *Die Tyrannis bei den Griechen* (2 vols., Munich 1967).

7 – C. G. Starr, *The Economic and Social Growth of Early Greece 800–500 BC* (New York 1977), pp. 16–17. In his notes Starr regularly praises as 'balanced' any work that persistently takes an on-the-one-hand-on-the-other-hand view of all theoretical positions and generalizations.

8 – I have tried briefly to restate the problem of the consumer-city in an additional chapter I have written for a new edition of *The Ancient Economy* (1985), and I shall

not return to the subject here beyond mentioning the critique of the concept of the ancient consumer-city by P. Leveau and the reply by C. Goudineau, in *Etudes rurales*, nos. 89–91 (1983) 275–89.

9 – W. J. Mommsen, *Max Weber, Gesellschaft, Politik und Geschichte* (Frankfurt 1974), pp. 224–5. Cf. P. Anderson, *Lineages of the Absolutist State* (London 1974), p. 410n22, about the 'increasing formalism of his later work' and the absence of 'any *historical* theory proper after his pioneering early work on Antiquity'.

10 – The subject is contentious: see the differences in nuance between Mommsen, *ibid.*, pp. 197–217, 224–32, and J. Kocka, 'Kontroversen über Max Weber', *Neue politische Literatur* 21 (1976) 281–301, at pp. 283–92.

11 – For references, see D. Roussel, *Tribu et cité* (*Annales . . . Besançon* 193, 1976), pp. 3–25.

12 – Weber, 'Agrarverhältnisse im Altertum', in his *Gesammelte Aufsätze zur Sozial- und Wirtschaftsgeschichte* (Tübingen 1924), pp. 1–288, at pp. 95–97; *Wirtschaft und Gesellschaft*, 5 ed. by J. Winckelmann (Tübingen 1972), pp. 219, 769.

13 – V. Ehrenberg, *L'état grec*, trans. C. Picavet-Roos, ed. E. Will (the latest ed. of a book originally publ. in German in 1932, Paris 1976), p. 37; Hasebroek, *Wirtschafts-geschichte*, esp. pp. 90–100.

14 – F. Cassola, *La Ionia nel mondo miceneo* (Naples 1957), pp. 246–56; A. Andrewes, 'Phratries in Homer', *Hermes* 99 (1961) 129–40.

15 – Roussel, *Tribu*; cf. F. Bourriot, *Recherches sur la nature du genos* (2 vols., Paris 1976).

16 – *Revue historique* 259 (1978) 509–15.

17 – Weber, *Wirtschaft*, pp. 240 and 238, resp.

18 – Weber himself attempted no more than that, in a few subtle pages: *ibid.*, pp. 235–42.

19 – It is enough to cite H. J. Wolff, 'Die Grundlagen des griechischen Eherechts', *Tijdschrift voor Rechtsgeschiedenis* 20 (1952) 1–54. I have protested against the idea of a single unified Greek law, in 'The Problem of the Unity of Greek Law', in my *Use and Abuse of History* (London and New York 1975), pp. 134–52, but I must concede that the specialists in Greek law have on the whole dismissed my arguments.

20 – R. J. Littman, 'Kinship in Athens', *Ancient Society* 10 (1979) 5–31.

21 – See e.g. W. J. Mommsen, *The Age of Bureaucracy* (Oxford 1974), pp. 15–17. It will spare some readers considerable effort in tracking down certain quotes from Weber if I give details of publication on this topic. The last account of legitimate domination that Weber himself prepared for publication appears in Part I of *Wirtschaft*, pp. 122–76. The long chap. 9 of that work (pp. 541–868) has been assembled by the editor from both published and unpublished material. There is also a posthumous article, 'Die drei reinen Typen der legitimen Herrschaft', published by his widow in *Preussische Jahrbücher* 187 (1922) 1–22, which the editor of *Wirtschaft* wrongly incorporated into the 4th ed. and then removed from the 5th (transferring it to the 3rd ed. of *Wissenschaftslehre*). A protest against the editor's manipulation of Weber's posthumous papers has been made by T. Schieder, in *Geschichte in Wissenschaft und Unterricht* 9 (1958) 649–54, and more than once by W. J. Mommsen, e.g. in *Historische Zeitschrift* 211 (1970) 616–18.

22 – *Wirtschaft*, p. 156.

23 – Quoted from the reprint in *Wissenschaftslehre*, p. 483.

24 – *Wirtschaft*, pp. 780–83. At one point (p. 783) the Athenian demagogue of the

Periclean age is said to be neither 'legitimate nor even legal' because his authority rested only on 'personal influence and the trust of the demos'. I am incapable of reconciling this with the discussion of charisma elsewhere.

25 – That is specifically said in *ibid.*, p. 156.

26 – Mommsen, *Bureaucracy*, pp. 83–5. Cf. J. G. Merquior, *Rousseau and Weber* (London and Boston 1980), ch. 7.

27 – Finley, 'Athenian Demagogues', *Past and Present* 21 (1962) 3–24, reprinted in the 2nd ed. of my *Democracy Ancient and Modern* (New Brunswick and London 1985).

28 – Mommsen, *Bureaucracy*, p. 88.

29 – W. Hennis, 'Zum Problem der deutschen Staatsanschauung', *Vierteljahrschrifte für Zeitgeschichte* 7 (1959) 3–23. It is worth stressing that Mommsen cites this article repeatedly, and with basic approval.

30 – O. Hintze, 'Max Weber's Soziologie', *Schmollers Jahrbuch* 50 (1926) 83–95; O. Brunner, 'Bemerkungen zu den Begriffer "Herrschaft" und "Legitimität"', in *Festschrift für Hans Sedlmayr* (Munich 1962), pp. 116–33.

31 – See the long postscript (pp. 442–77) in the second ed. (1974).

32 – Mommsen, *Bureaucracy*, p. 114*n*25.

33 – See Q. Skinner, 'The Empirical Theorists of Democracy and Their Critics', *Political Theory* 1 (1973) 287–305.

34 – *Democracy*, chap. 1.

35 – Mommsen, *Bureaucracy*, p. 80.

36 – *Wirtschaft*, pp. 155–6. The German is extremely difficult: 'Denn die tatsächliche Geltung der charismatischen Autorität ruht in der Tat gänzlich auf der durch "Bewährung" bedingten *Anerkennung* durch die Beherrschten . . .' Mommsen, *Bureaucracy*, p. 90, translates: 'In fact, the leader (demagogue) rules by virtue of the devotion (of his followers) and their confidence in him as a person.'

37 – *Gesammelte Aufsätze zur Religionssoziologie* (repr. Tübingen 1934) I 2 and 11.

38 – *Wirtschaft*, p. 455; cf. 505.

39 – The phrase is that of Hans Julius Wolff, the best and most influential student of Greek law in our time: 'Griechische Rechtsgeschichte als Anliegen der Altertumswissenschaft und der Rechtswissenschaft', in his *Opuscula dispersa* (Amsterdam 1974), pp. 15–25.

40 – The best work was in French, and I see no evidence that Weber knew it or indeed anything important in German other than Mitteis' *Reichsrecht und Volksrecht*, the central concern of which was the later Roman Empire, not the Greek city-states.

41 – *Wirtschaft*, p. 158.

42 – *Ibid.*, p. 810.

43 – Note the frequency with which this is pointed out in one way or another in Max Rheinstein's notes in his valuable English edition, *Max Weber on Law and Society* (Cambridge, Mass., 1954).

44 – E.g. *Wirtschaft*, pp. 470–71, 510, 563–4.

45 – *Ibid.*, pp. 563–4.

46 – For a recent statement by a legal historian, see M. Talamanca in *Il diritto in Grecia e a Roma*, by M. Bretone and Talamanca (Bari 1981), pp. 19–29.

47 – *Wirtschaft*, p. 158.

48 – *Ibid.*, pp. 464–7.

49 – *Ibid.*, p. 564.

50 – For a radical reinterpretation of Hammurabi and his 'code' (a mistaken label), see now J. Bottéro, in *Annali . . . Pisa*, 3rd ser., 12 (1982) 409–44.

51 – Weber, *Wirtschaft*, p. 158, wrote that the only Roman analogy to these Athenian forensic speeches is to be found in Cicero's speeches in political trials, but that is unfair because there is no parallel anywhere to the literary genre of the Athenian forensic oration. Hence there is no basis for judging whether the behaviour of Athenian advocates was or was not unique.

52 – See my *Politics*, pp. 135–41.

53 – See especially H. Meyer-Laurin, *Gesetz und Billigkeit im attischen Prozess* (Weimar 1965); J. Meinecke, 'Gesetzesinterpretation und Gesetzesanwendung im attischen Zivilprozess', *Revue internationale des droits de l'antiquité*, 3rd ser., 18 (1971) 275–360.

54 – D. Cohen, *Theft in Athenian Law* (*Münchener Beiträge* 74, 1983), esp. the Prolegomena; Finley, *Land and Credit* (3:33), esp. pp. 113–17.

55 – L. Gernet, 'L'institution des arbitres publics à Athènes', *Revue des études grecques* 52 (1939) 389–414, reprinted in his *Droit et société dans la Grèce ancienne* (repr., Paris 1955), pp. 103–19, at p. 114.

56 – The fundamental study remains A. Steinwenter, *Die Streitbeendigung durch Urteil, Schiedspruch und Vergleich nach griechischem Rechte* (*Münchener Beiträge* 8, 1925).

57 – Modern jurists have made heavy weather with this text, including S. Huwardas, who in the end produces the correct, straightforward explanation: 'Über die Vergleiche und die privaten Schiedsprüche nach attischem Rechte', *Zeitschrift für vergleichende Rechtswissenschaft* 49 (1939) 289–335, at pp. 311–21.

58 – Gernet, *op. cit.*, p. 113.

Index

Compiled by Douglas Matthews